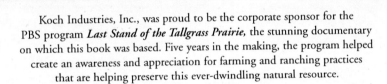

Koch Industries, Inc., was proud to be the corporate sponsor for the PBS program *Last Stand of the Tallgrass Prairie*, the stunning documentary on which this book was based. Five years in the making, the program helped create an awareness and appreciation for farming and ranching practices that are helping preserve this ever-dwindling natural resource.

Rooted in Fred Koch's love for the Flint Hills, Koch has a long-standing commitment to the environment. We hope the small part Koch played in this project will help ensure the preservation of this valuable land for hundreds of years.

It is our hope that *Last Stand of the Tallgrass Prairie* will stimulate your personal interest in the beauty, culture, and environmental significance of this unique ecosystem.

KOCH
INDUSTRIES INC

last stand of the tallgrass prairie

last stand of the tallgrass prairie

Aimée Larrabee and John Altman

FRIEDMAN/FAIRFAX
PUBLISHERS

A FRIEDMAN/FAIRFAX BOOK
Please visit our website: www.metrobooks.com

Library of Congress Cataloging-in-Publication Data

Larrabee, Aimee.
   The last stand of the tall grass prairie / Aimee Larrabee and John Altman.
      p. cm.
   Includes bibliographical references.
   ISBN 1-58663-134-9 (alk. paper)
    1. Prairie ecology—United States. 2. Praries—United States. 3. Prairies--United States—History. I. Altman, John. II. Title.

   QH104 .L33 2001
   577.4'4'0973--dc21
00-049481

Editor: Susan Lauzau
Art Director: Jeff Batzli
Designer: Lynne Yeamans
Photo Editor: Kate Perry
Production Manager: Richela Fabian Morgan

Color separations by Fine Arts Repro House Co., Ltd.
Printed in Spain by Book Print, S.L.

10 9 8 7 6 5 4 3 2 1

Distributed by Sterling Publishing Company, Inc.
387 Park Avenue South
New York, NY 10016
Distributed in Canada by Sterling Publishing
Canadian Manda Group
One Atlantic Avenue, Suite 105
Toronto, Ontario, Canada M6K 3E7
Distributed in Australia by
Capricorn Link (Australia) Pty Ltd.
P.O. Box 6651
Baulkham Hills, Business Centre, NSW 2153, Australia

dedication

We dedicate this book to Kate and Tim Larrabee, who saw this land with the purity of a child's eyes, finding wonder in its simplicity, peace in its vast horizons, and pure exhilaration in its beckoning hills.

acknowledgments

Many special thanks go to Kristin Frizzell, our researcher, who spent countless hours digging into the history of this beautiful place, and to David Hartnett, Alan Knapp, and John Blair, from Kansas State University and the Konza Prairie Biological Station, who demonstrated to us how the beauty of the prairie can be perceived through the rigorous discipline of Science. A special thanks also to Lyle Lovett, who lent his voice and his warmth to the project, and to Michael Murphy, a great person who deeply enhanced the final product.

Our heartfelt thanks go also to the generous and inspiring men and women who shared with us their love and respect for this peaceful place on earth:

Joe Williams, Michael Lucio and family, Tom Ross, Tom Sanders, Jeffrey Standing Bear, and Jerry Flute, who helped nurture in us an appreciation of the mystical bond between Native Americans and their Mother Earth;

Maggie and Bill Haw, Rose and Kent Bacon, Carl Grunder, Tim and Trey Miser, Jeannie and Tom Cernich, and Dee and Fred Lyons, whose stewardship goes far beyond the economic well-being of their ranching operations;

Tom Van Slyke, Phil Fay, Rosemary Ramundo, Gail Wilson, and Valerie Wright, who guided us through the daily rigors of research at the Konza Prairie; Susan Barnes of the Grand Central Hotel and Dianna Carlson of the Cassoday Café, whose Flint Hills hospitality made our days there ones we will always cherish; and Bob Krause, Paul Lowe, and their staffs at Kansas State University for putting the strength of their great organization behind our efforts.

And finally to our editor Susan Lauzau, art director Jeff Batzli, and photo editor Kate Perry, whose perspicacity is exceeded only by their persistence. And to Linda Nagy who held the project together beautifully. And to Mark and Kristine for their support.

contents

When I first met writer/filmmaker John Altman, he told me the story of how his partner, Aimée Larrabee, suggested that they make a film about the tallgrass prairie. "You want to make a film about grass growing?" was John's reply. "Maybe next we can do one on paint drying." Times were tough in the documentary filmmaking world, and in-your-face shaky-cam reporting on gutsy subjects had found its place in the American psyche. But John's a nice guy, so he drove with Aimée the two hours from their office in Kansas City to the place of her life-long affection, a little-known swath of ground called the Flint Hills of Kansas.

That was five years and dozens of filming trips ago. That was before the National Science Foundation, the Environmental Protection Agency, and the National Endowment for the Arts teamed up with private foundations and corporate America to fund their film on grass. Before the Smithsonian Institution and this book publisher would all agree that grass was not only a breathtakingly beautiful subject, but a terribly important one as well. That was before I met them, but not before I understood the peace that such a vast, open space could bring. I was happy to lend my voice to helping city dwellers around the world come to a deeper realization that since humans first began to hunt and then to plow the land, we have always been first and foremost people of the grass.

America's prairie once covered the middle third of our continent. Now, almost all of it is gone. Tallgrass prairie, in fact, is the most endangered ecosystem in North America, with less than 5 percent of its original stretches remaining. Scientists are spending a great deal of time studying what's left, as it has important ramifications for both the food we eat and the air we breathe.

John and Aimée met a great many people during their treks through this grassland: scientists from grasslands around the globe, traveling to Kansas to study the ecosystem; cowboys; Indians; ranchers; poets. Poets who were ranchers; scientists who were cowboys; buffalo lovers and wildflower gurus. Still photographers and painters. Native American spiritual leaders and potluck supper clubs in towns of two hundred. They quote Willa Cather, Thomas Hart Benton, and William Inge. They both truly love the place. And when it comes time to sum up the overall experience of spending time in one of the few places in America where you can turn a camera 360 degrees and see no sign of human existence in any direction, they quote a banker-turned-land manager they met along their journey: "You can say it in four words: 'Good for the soul.'"

Over time, this prairie has been home to scores of Native American tribes, then waves of homesteaders. There have been bloody clashes over its incredibly fertile loam and volumes have been written on its subtle beauty. What was once prairie is now mostly highways and cities. Native grasses have been turned over to domesticated ones. What remains is truly a beautiful spot on Earth, worthy of close, loving examination. That's why I got involved. This is a compelling story of science, indeed, but mostly, it's a story of people and their connection to a very special place. It's about people who feel their souls in a stretch of land.

Welcome to the land of tall grasses.

INTRODUCTION

The sound of the grasslands is the earth's eternal lullaby. Gentle, swaying, soft, and comforting, the grasses whisper in the wind, swaddling myriad forms of life within their golden waves and throughout their intricate root systems. Deer mice, voles, and hundreds of species of insects make the grasses pulse with life.

For thousands of years, the grasses on the prairies—North America's native grasslands—have absorbed the energy of the sun and converted it into carbohydrates, proteins, fats, and vitamins, which are consumed by grazing animals. In prehistoric times these animals were mammoths and musk oxen, later they were bison, then cattle. The nutrients passed on to us as we hunted and ate the animals fed by the grasses. We even began cultivating this life-giving energy more directly, as we developed and grew grasses we could eat, like corn, wheat, soy, and others. As a species we flourished.

Today, we are discovering that much of the excess carbon dioxide being pumped into the air by our burning of fossil fuels is pulled out daily by grasses—both wild and domestic—and deposited into the soil. In a blessed paradox, what was once pollution becomes food for the grasses, and thus, eventually, for humans. No matter who we are or where we live, our lives still depend largely on our grasslands—for our crops, for our beef, and even for the purity of our air.

Yet the grasslands—the ancestral home of our species and our greatest hope for continued survival—are now among the most threatened biomes in the world. The tallgrass prairie is the most endangered ecosystem in North America, with less than 5 percent remaining. To save our native grasslands, we must understand the workings of those that remain and how to best manage the acreage that has been converted to cropland. Long-range, scientific studies being conducted deep in America's heartland, at Kansas State University's Konza Prairie Research Natural Area, are providing detailed information on everything from microbial life forms to large grazers, offering a deeper understanding of the magnificent workings of this ecosystem. This knowledge, we must all hope, will help us in our continued fight for the last stand of the tallgrass prairie.

OPPOSITE: *A pair of dragonflies display their delicately veined wings in the tallgrass of Minnesota.* **RIGHT:** *Grasses have helped humans sustain life for millennia, providing food directly in the form of edible grassses like wheat and corn, and indirectly by nourishing bison, cattle, and other grazers that we then consume.*

CHAPTER ONE

the sea of grass

Seventy million years ago, the North American prairies did not exist. At that time, the Rocky Mountains had not yet formed, and North America was forested from coast to coast. Shifts in the huge plates that make up the earth's surface, followed by changes in temperature and rainfall, began the creation of the most fertile grasslands on the planet; the place we now know as the tallgrass prairie.

Once a vast, steamy, inland sea with marshy shores and dense surrounds of tropical forests, North America was populated over successive epochs by everything from crustaceans and primitive fishes to dinosaurs. As the continent swelled and shrank, heaved and receded, it passed through the millennia without the presence of the human species.

By the time the first humans ventured onto the continent some twelve thousand years ago, the dinosaurs were long gone. The ice that had covered everything melted, receded, and froze over again and again, leaving in its wake gigantic mementos of the geologic upheaval caused by the powerful combination of water and hugely fluctuating temperatures. Born were the Rocky Mountains in ranges in the land's central western area, blocks of towering peaks that captured and redirected the air as it streamed over the land from warm western shores. The new, more arid climate on the eastern side of the mountains favored the deep-rooted, drought-tolerant grasses, which took hold and began to move eastward. The grasslands gradually expanded, helped by wind, which carried grass seeds far and wide; by fire, which destroyed swathes of forest,

LEFT: *In late autumn, Konza Prairie's vast stretch of grasses shimmers with gold. It is this view of boundless, undulating waves of grasses—together with its historical watery past—that led to the description of the prairie as an "inland sea."*

RIGHT: *Thickspike gayfeather (Liatris pycnostachya), also called prairie blazing star, flourishes in the moist, open lands of the eastern prairie, where rainfall is relatively high. The tall plumes of this perennial are perfect anchors for the gossamer strands of a thousand spiderwebs.*

offering grasses fertile new territory; and by large prehistoric mammals, whose grazing stimulated each plant's growth, much like careful pruning.

The scant rainfall on the western plains caused the grasses there to be relatively short, but the winds that crossed the continent picked up new moisture coming down from Canada and up from the Gulf of Mexico. The grasses grew higher and higher: the tallgrass prairie was being formed.

But wind and rainfall were not the only factors that created the prairies; glaciers, too, did their part to shape the land. These massive ice flows smoothed the tracts of earth they traveled over, creating level plains. As the glaciers advanced and retreated and advanced again, they left deposits of rich glacial soil, which ultimately became the fertile soil of America's breadbasket.

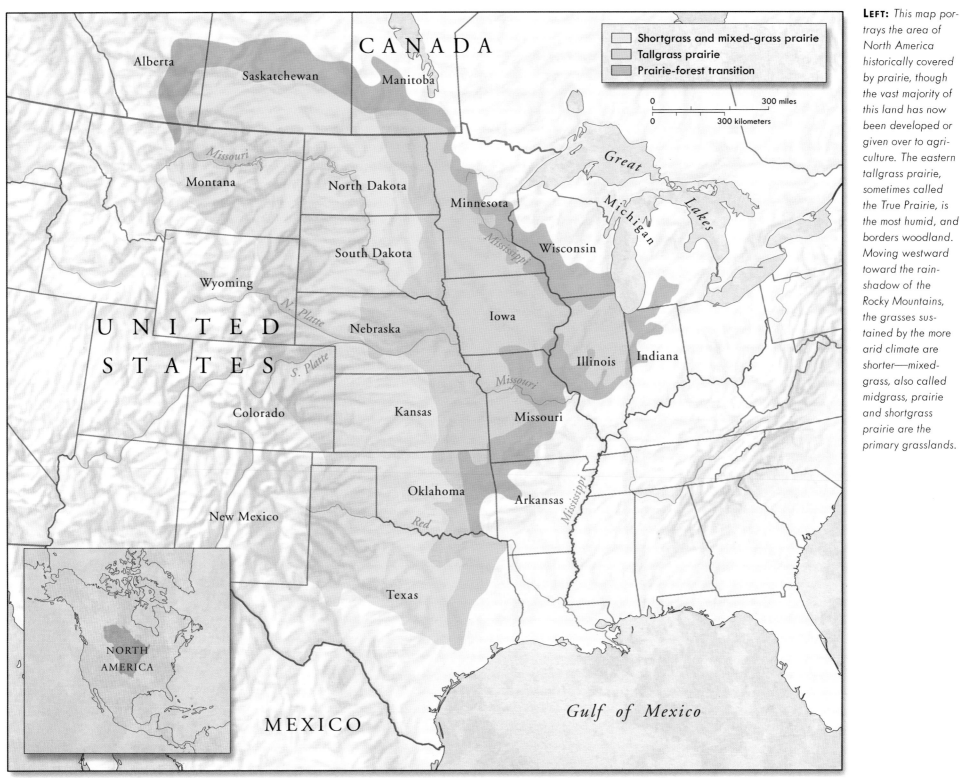

Shortgrass and mixed-grass prairie
Tallgrass prairie
Prairie-forest transition

CANADA

Alberta
Saskatchewan
Manitoba

UNITED STATES

Montana

North Dakota

Minnesota

Great Lakes

Michigan

South Dakota

Wisconsin

Wyoming

Iowa

Nebraska

Illinois

Indiana

Colorado

Kansas

Missouri

New Mexico

Oklahoma

Arkansas

Texas

NORTH AMERICA

MEXICO

Gulf of Mexico

Missouri
Mississippi
N. Platte
S. Platte
Red

0   300 miles
0   300 kilometers

LEFT: *This map portrays the area of North America historically covered by prairie, though the vast majority of this land has now been developed or given over to agriculture. The eastern tallgrass prairie, sometimes called the True Prairie, is the most humid, and borders woodland. Moving westward toward the rain-shadow of the Rocky Mountains, the grasses sustained by the more arid climate are shorter—mixed-grass, also called midgrass, prairie and shortgrass prairie are the primary grasslands.*

OPPOSITE: *The small, rosy pink blooms of prairie smoke (Geum triflorum)* ultimately open to release the plant's namesake seedheads, which look like airy plumes of smoke.
LEFT: *Milkweed (Asclepias spp.)* seedlings take to the prairie winds. Wind has been a major factor in shaping this ecosystem since the prairie's formation millions of years ago.

Anatomy of a Grass

The prairies are dominated by grasses, and indeed almost a third of the earth is covered by grass. There are some 9,700 species of grass on earth. They occur on all continents from the Arctic to the Sub-Antarctic and are distributed over a wide range of habitats. They hold the hills and plains against the destructive forces of erosion by wind and water. Pastures feed our livestock, and grain, paper, spices, and oils, together with hundreds of other items in daily use, are products of grasses. Grasses were the first plants to be cultivated as food, and most of the dozen or so crops that feed the world today are grasses. Although immensely common and tremendously important, this is the group of plants perhaps least understood and least appreciated by the casual observer. What is a grass, and what distinguishes grasses from other plants?

Botanists classify groups of plants with similar characteristics into families. Grasses are members of the plant family Poaceae, one of many families of flowering plants. Their classification as flowering plants is noteworthy, as one of the common misconceptions about grasses is that they have no flowers. Grasses do have flowers, just as sunflowers and goldenrods and roses do; the only difference is that the flowers of grasses are small and inconspicuous, and differ slightly in structure. Unlike flowering plants that produce showy, colorful, and fragrant flowers to attract animal pollinators, a grass is structurally adapted for pollination by the wind. The flowers of a grass are arranged on the stalks in two rows. Each of the tiny flowers, borne singly or in groups within this spikelet, is enclosed within small scale-like structures called bracts. In addition to reproducing via flowers and seed, grasses may reproduce vegetatively, producing new shoots or tillers from underground horizontal creeping stems called stolens or rhizomes, or from a dense crown at the base of the plant.

In addition to their small inconspicuous flowers, grass plants are characterized by long

narrow leaves with parallel veins. The stems are usually round and mainly hollow, except at the node, the point where the leaf is attached to the stem. The stems have joints, noticeable bulges where the leaves are attached. The base of the leaf wraps around the stem in a structure called the sheath. Thus, they contrast strongly with many other flowering plants that have broad leaves with branching veins that are attached to a stem by a small stalk or petiole.

Although the basic structure of the leaf, stem, and flowers are similar among grasses, different grass species vary considerably and can be recognized based on differences in the bracts surrounding the flowers, the ways in which flower spikelets are grouped into clusters, or inflorescences, and the overall architecture or growth form of the entire plant. Growth form variation among grasses originates from the patterns of growth and development of new young shoots, or tillers. In some species, many new tillers emerge directly from within the leaf sheaths at the base of the plant, producing a "bunchgrass" growth form. In others, extensive lateral growth of rhizomes or stolons produces new tillers at their tips, resulting in a widely spreading or "sodgrass" growth form.

In contrast to many other plants, the growing points, or meristems, of grasses are protected, located down low near the base of the plant, rather than at the tips of the stems and branches. Thus, if the plant is grazed by an animal or otherwise damaged, the growing points or buds remain unharmed and it can easily regrow. In addition, grasses maintain a large amount of roots and rhizomes belowground to store food reserves for regrowth. As a result, in some cases the stems and leaves we see aboveground comprise less than one-fifth of the weight of the entire grass plant. These two traits of grasses help explain their tremendous resiliency to aboveground damage, and their excellent adaptation to drought, fire, grazing, and mowing.

—*D. C. Hartnett*

BELOW: *Little bluestem (Andropogon scoparius) was, historically, the most abundant of the prairie grasses.* **OPPOSITE:** *Mixed tall-grasses show the plants' ability to bend and sway with the wind.*

RIGHT: *Formed between fourteen thousand and twenty-four thousand years ago, Iowa's Loess Hills, north of Sioux City, are creations of wind and water. In warm weather, glacier melt caused powerful flows of water to run down the river valleys, but in cooler weather, the melt slowed or stopped, revealing enormous mud flats. Winds then blew over the exposed sediment, picking up and depositing the finer particles in the bluffs that exist there today.*

OPPOSITE: *Trees, like this solitary cottonwood, merely dot the horizon or line streambanks. A healthy prairie has a limited number of trees or other woody plants.*

Grasslands require a simple but important combination of three key factors in order to survive: a temperate climate, the grazing of large animals, and widespread, intermittent fires. In North America, the dominant grazers were once bison but have been replaced largely by cattle; on other continents, grazers include yak, wildebeest, zebra, and impala, as well as cattle.

Aside from stimulating plant growth by eating grass tops, the grazers provide important nutrients for the plants and the soil in the form of urine and dung, which contain highly concentrated nitrogen in a readily accessible state. Nitrogen, a component of all proteins, is an essential building block of every living plant and animal.

Fire helps maintain productive grassland by removing dead plant material from above ground, allowing the sun to warm the soil surface and promote new growth. It also removes from the tallgrass prairie what grassland ecologists call "woody invaders." Better known as trees and shrubs, these plants overwhelm grasslands unless they are kept in check by fire, which kills woody plants because the majority of their growth tissue is aboveground and is therefore consumed by flames. Grasslands, conversely, can be thought of as "upside-down forests," because about two-thirds of their mass and their buds grow below the ground, and are thus fire resistant.

Lightning was nature's first line of defense in keeping grasslands healthy. A single strike might cause a fire that could burn uninterrupted for miles and continue for days. But within a week after a burn, tender new shoots emerged from the charred earth. It is this simple system that serves the human species in more ways than one.

Living Life at Many Levels

Like ecosystems all across the globe, the prairie functions at many different levels: birds and insects on the wing fill the air, large mammals tread the ground, small mammals and reptiles scurry among the grasses and burrow beneath the earth, and other insects, earthworms, and microbes live deep within the soil. This mural, part of the Smithsonian Institution's exhibit "Listening to the Prairie: Farming in Nature's Image," illustrates the complexity of life on the prairies. Some of the more than forty species of wildlife to be found in this image include:

- Bison
- Red fox
- Badger
- Deer mouse
- Prairie vole
- Eastern cottontail rabbit
- Coyote
- White-tailed deer
- Upland sandpiper
- Black rat snake
- Western box turtle
- Red-winged blackbird
- Prairie chicken
- Earthworm
- Monarch butterfly

Mural by Hugh McKay, McKay/Scheer Studios, Washington, DC. © Smithsonian Institution, 2000.

The Role of Fire in Tallgrass Prairie

Periodic fires played an important role in the history of tallgrass prairies. Although fires can occur in virtually any grassland, from arid desert grasslands to lush tallgrass prairies, the frequency and importance of fire varies with average annual rainfall and the productivity of the grassland. In North America, tallgrass prairies occur in the transition zone, or ecotone, between the wetter deciduous forests to the east and the more arid shortgrass prairies and desert grasslands to the south and west. Because of the relatively high rainfall, they include some of the most productive grasslands in North America. The high productivity and annual growth of the grasses allow for the buildup of fine, combustible fuel in the form of dead grass (detritus), and so fires were believed to have been widespread and common throughout the history of these grasslands. Lightning was probably a common source of ignition for these fires, although it also is likely that early native Americans started fires for a variety of reasons, including clearing detritus and attracting bison to areas of grass regrowth. Fire also plays an essential part in the management of present-day tallgrass prairies, where it is used by land managers and ranchers to limit the growth of woody plants and to promote the growth and vigor of the dominant warm-season grasses, like big bluestem (*Andropogon gerardii*) and Indian grass (*Sorghastrum nutans*).

An important effect of fire in tallgrass prairie is to limit the encroachment of woody plants. Tallgrass prairies occur in areas where rainfall is sufficient to support the growth of woody plants, such as smooth sumac and red cedar. In the absence of periodic fires, shrubs and trees would eventually replace the grasses and wildflowers characteristic of tallgrass

BELOW: *Flames consume dead grass, leaving the blackened earth to accept the sun's rays more directly. As a result, soil temperatures rise, stimulating plant growth.* **OPPOSITE:** *An elm tree is silhouetted by an evening prairie fire.*

prairie. However, shrubs and trees have sensitive growing tissues located at the tips of their branches, which can be easily damaged in the heat of prairie fire. Grasses, in contrast, have their growing points protected belowground, and are capable of rapid regrowth after a fire. Thus, frequent fires are essential for maintaining these ecosystems as grasslands.

In addition to preventing the growth of woody plants, fire can affect the growth and composition of herbaceous prairie plants. Spring fires generally increase the total plant productivity of the prairie by stimulating growth of the warm-season grasses. This results from the removal of the large amount of plant detritus that accumulates in the absence of the fire. This detritus acts as a mulch layer, keeping soils cool in the spring and limiting light availability for emerging plants. The removal of the detritus and standing dead plants alters the energy environment and microclimate of the soil, allowing the soil to warm much more quickly in the spring. These changes in the soil microclimate promote the rapid growth and development of the dominant warm-season grasses. The increased growth of the grasses also increases their ability to compete with other plant species, leading to another effect of frequent fires—a reduction in the abundance and diversity of some nongrass prairie plants, including some of the wildflowers that contribute to the biodiversity of tallgrass prairies. Thus, frequent burning increases plant productivity, but can also reduce plant diversity, at least in ungrazed prairie. However, by controlling the timing and frequency of fires, and through controlled grazing or mowing, both the diversity and integrity of prairies can be maintained.

—*John Blair*

RIGHT: *Before cities and highways were built, creating barriers to the spread of prairie fires, these lightning-ignited blazes could burn unchecked for days on end, covering miles of ground and encompassing several modern-day counties. At night, the fires become a crackling show of light on the vast horizon, burning in a series of thin, wind-directed lines.*

Native grasses, like the prairie's big bluestem, are perennials that grow in open grasslands, but domesticated species, like rice and corn, are annual agricultural crops that feed the world. Deep inside their plant tissues and roots, the millennia-old native grasses carry secrets to superior drought tolerance and pest and disease resistance, secrets that, if unraveled, could be extremely valuable to farmers growing the native grasses' domesticated cousins. Ultimately, the lessons learned from the native grasses may cut the use of herbicides and pesticides on our own food crops.

Grasslands also purify the air we breathe through photosynthesis, the conversion of sunlight into chemical energy. All green plants engage in this natural process. In so doing, they supply the energy they need to live, but help other living things as well, by taking carbon dioxide from the atmosphere and releasing oxygen in its place. They then convert carbon dioxide into new plant tissues. In the case of the grasses, a large portion of these tissues are in the form of roots that stretch deep below the earth's surface, releasing and storing organic matter and nutrient minerals into the surrounding soil. Dig deep into a segment of what remains of North America's tallgrass prairie, and you'll find very dark, carbon-rich and nutrient-laden soil, a most hospitable medium for native and cultivated species of grass.

In millennia gone by, soil enriching was a major benefit of this carbon sequestration. But that was before we began burning fossil fuels by the ton, emitting carbon dioxide, one of the greenhouse gases (so called because of their heat-trapping properties), into the atmosphere at such a rate that the cleansing processes of nature couldn't keep up. And, in our rush to "civilize" the land, we in North America dug up much of our grasslands, thus removing a huge natural air purifier.

From Sunlight to Sustenance

Earth's atmosphere contains less than 0.05% carbon dioxide, yet it is this inorganic carbon that provides the building blocks for 99.5% of all life on earth. Driven by energy from the sun, plants remove carbon dioxide from the atmosphere and, through the process of photosynthesis, create forms of organic carbon such as sugars, starch, and cellulose. Along the way, water molecules are split and oxygen is released as a byproduct.

Prairie plants are particularly good at the process of photosynthesis, especially the warm-season grasses such as big bluestem and Indian grass. As a result, tallgrass prairie is one of the most productive grassland types in North America. The abundance of organic carbon—the plants themselves—is clearly evident aboveground. It is this energy source that sustained the historically large bison herds as well as the carnivores that fed on these and other herbivores. However, in tallgrass prairie, even more carbon is stored belowground in plant roots and rhizomes (underground stems). As much as two to four times more plant biomass may occur below the soil surface than aboveground. This prairie plant strategy of placing essential carbon belowground ensures the survival of the vegetation in the face of fire, drought, and grazing (although grazing belowground by insects and myriad other small creatures can also be substantial).

One result of this belowground carbon allocation strategy is that as plant parts die and decompose, the most decay-resistant parts build up in the soil as persistent organic matter. Over thousands of years, these production and decay processes led to the creation of the organic matter-rich or "black" soils characteristic of tallgrass prairie. Ironically, it was the presence of these fertile soils, which also contained abundant organic nitrogen, that made the tallgrass prairie so attractive to early farmers, speeding the land's conversion to row-crop agriculture. Today, agricultural scientists recognize the immense value of maintaining high soil quality for sustaining crop production. Indeed, building and maintaining soil quality in croplands similar to that found in grasslands is a management goal that has proven difficult to achieve. But in the tallgrass prairie, building high-quality soil is a natural outcome of the way this ecosystem, led by its dominant grasses, processes energy.

—Alan Knapp

RIGHT: *Like green plants the world over, big bluestem (Andropogon gerardii) uses light energy to convert water, carbon dioxide, and minerals drawn from the earth into proteins, fats, vitamins, and other organic compounds. An important byproduct of this process, called photosynthesis, is oxygen.*

BELOW: *True North American natives, sunflowers dot the prairie landscape, sharing the soils harmoniously with indigenous grasses.* **OPPOSITE:** *Humans have known since they first settled on the prairies in pre-historic times that the soils created by the native grasses make superb farmland. Today, the vast majority of what was once North American prairie has been converted to row crop agriculture.*

Ironically, we first began releasing large quantities of greenhouse gases into the environment in our desire to turn native grassland, which we thought of as useless, into valuable cropland, which could be used to feed the country. The simple act of turning over the soil—plowing the grass under—in such large quantities created the first appreciable increase in carbon dioxide released into the atmosphere. This historic increase seems to have begun at about the same time the prairies began disappearing, around 1850. But we've far exceeded our own record in decades since.

Today, our planet's industrialized societies release an average of 7,400 million metric tons of carbon into the air every day. Because of environmental indicators such as increased global temperatures and ozone depletion, many scientists fear that we are compromising our planet's ability to regulate the composition of its atmosphere and the range of its temperatures. How far can we tip this delicate global balance before there are serious consequences for all life on earth?

The earth's landscapes, atmosphere, and temperature have always shifted, but normally over very long periods of time—not over a mere 150 years, the period during which the most recent radical changes have been wrought. In order to look forward and understand how to preserve, and perhaps even recover, some of the precious gifts of the prairies, we must first look back, to a time when humans first began to manipulate this environment, to look for shelter and sustenance in a new-found land—the land of tall grasses.

Wildlife in the Tallgrass

While the prairie appears to be a waving sea of grass, grass, and nothing but grass, among the grasses nearly eight hundred species of mammals, birds, reptiles, and amphibians thrive. The tallgrass prairie, with its location in the center of the continent, is a coming-together point for North American animals. From the mighty bison to the tiny vole, the animals of the prairie are supported and nurtured by the grasses. The plant population, while not as diverse, exits in major groupings of flowers called "forbs" that dot the horizon in a seasonal display of color. Additional color comes from a variety of legumes, which provide nutrients to the soil, a benefit to the grasses that share the rich loam.

CLOCKWISE FROM LEFT: *Hundreds of species of grasshoppers alone demonstrate the important role of insects in the prairie; white-tailed deer, like this eleven-point buck, thrive in the prairie ecosystem; prairie chickens are most graceful dancers in spring's mating season; jackrabbits must be ever watchful for potential predators like hawks and coyotes.*

RIGHT: *In June, butterfly milk-weed (Ascelpias tuberosa) draws butterflies and other nectar lovers to its bright orange clusters.*

Far right: *The leaves of big bluestem (Andropogon gerardii) are bluish in color and turn reddish purple as the plant matures; it is the blue tones that give this native grass its name.*

RIGHT BOTTOM: *Side oats gramma (Bouteleua cur-tipendula) is one of the most delicate prairie grasses, with tiny flowers sus-pended from one side of its stem.*

FAR LEFT: *Wild blue indigo (Baptisia australis) is a member of the legume family, an important part of the prairie plant community.*
LEFT: *The compass plant (Silphium laciniatum) was so named because the edges of its leaves tend to point north and south, which helped to orient travelers.*
BELOW: *Purple coneflowers (Echinacea purpurea) are prairie natives whose seedheads provide food for birds; Plains Indians used this plant*

the first americans

At the start of the new millennium, we took stock of the past century, marveling at the everyday conveniences that were unavailable, indeed incomprehensible, to those alive when the last century was born. Cars, airplanes, skyscrapers, modern computers, fax machines, cell phones, televisions, air conditioning, microwave ovens…all are new in the last hundred years. In one lifetime, the world is a very different place.

In other lifetimes, other centuries, changes wrought by humans were not so fast in coming. Changes occurred gradually, sometimes over many millennia, but they did come. And the grasslands played a significant role in the changes humans would face, for it was on the wide-open grasslands that we began our long march toward dominance as a species.

Our distant ancestors climbed down from their safe perches in the trees and ventured out onto Africa's vast savannas in search of greater and more varied food sources—edible roots, berries, and small creatures. It is this move out of the trees that most scientists credit with the motivation toward bipedalism, our upright walking stance,

LEFT: *The first humans to reach the middle of North America found tracts of grassland interrupted periodically by a tree, stream, or rocky outcropping.*
ABOVE: *Many early communities settled near tree-lined water sources, but hunted in the open grasses. This archival photograph shows members of the Kansa people, circa 1872, who lived along the Kansas and Saline rivers.*

RIGHT:

Anthropologists speculate that large herds of grazing mammals feeding on the young grasslands of North America attracted hunters from other parts of the world over the Bering land bridges. This human migration began some twelve to fifteen thousand years ago, and archaeological evidence suggests that people had reached the prairies at least eleven thousand years ago.

The Prairies

These are the gardens of the Desert, these
The unshorn fields, boundless and beautiful
For which the speech of England has no name—
The Prairies, I behold them for the first,
And my heart swells, while the dilated sight
Takes in the encircling vastness.

—William Cullen Bryant

which allowed early humans to scan the horizon for danger and later for prey, and to carry foodstuffs and other objects easily.

As the millennia passed and our ancestors adapted to life on the savannas, they not only foraged for fruits, nuts, and the small creatures that hid in the dense grasses, they began to hunt for larger prey, targeting the grazing animals that roamed the savannas by the millions. Hunting large prey required more effort and organization, but also yielded greater rewards in the form of a sustained supply of protein and fat.

It is likely that the need to follow the herds is what first led humans into North America. While most Native Americans base their beliefs about the peopling of the continent on Origin Stories, in which their lives originated here, archaeological evidence suggests that sometime during the last Ice Age, perhaps twelve to fifteen thousand years ago, ancient Asiatic peoples traveled over the Bering land bridge into North America; others perhaps crossed the Pacific Ocean. Theirs were the first human feet to touch this place on earth. Thousands of years later, others would arrive from Europe bearing flags and weapons of war and declarations of discovery in the names of kings and queens. These humans would bring with them different concepts of ownership and imperial order, of possession and value.

Osage Creation Story

Most historians and scientists ascribe to the theory that humans inhabited the North American continent by crossing the Bering Sea via a land bridge created by falling sea levels during a period of intense glaciation. Native American societies explain their presence in this land through numerous creation stories that account for both the advent of humankind and their celestial journey to earth. The following story is from the Wazhazhe, or Osage, people.

Way beyond, a part of the Wazhazhe lived in the sky. They desired to know their origin, the source from which they came into existence. They went to the sun. He told them that they were his children. Then they wandered still farther and came to the moon. She told them that she gave birth to them, and that the sun was their father. She told them that they must leave their present abode and go down to the earth and dwell there. They came to the earth, but found it covered with water. The animal were with them, and of all these, the elk was the finest and most stately, and inspired all the creatures with confidence; so they appealed to the elk for help. He dropped into the water and began to sink. Then he called to the winds and the winds came from all quarters and blew until the waters went upward in a mist.

BELOW: Most Native American tribes believe that their people were placed on this land by the Creator.

At first rocks only were exposed, and the people traveled on the rocky places that produced no plants, and there was nothing to eat. Then the waters began to go down until the soft earth was exposed. When this happened the elk in his joy rolled over and over on the soft earth, and all his loose hairs clung to the soil. The hairs grew, and from them sprang beans, corn, potatoes, and wild turnips, and then all the grasses and trees.

Adapted from "The Omaha Tribe," Alice C. Fletcher and Francis La Flesche, *27th Annual Report of the Bureau of American Ethnology.*

But that was not the way of these first Americans. They hunted for a living, in the truest sense of the word, roaming the continent following the herds of large mammals that went where the forage was fresh and plentiful. The protein these people sought was in the form of moose and musk ox, mammoth and prehistoric bison, and the life-sustaining cycle was a simple one: the grazers ate grasses, rich in protein but inedible to humans, and the humans ate the meat of the grazers. The nutrients consumed by grazers were returned to the soil in urine and dung, to be used again by the grasses.

It was a cycle that defined every aspect of these humans' existence—where they lived, when and how they moved, why and how they developed weapons and tools. For generations to come it would be what they sang about and prayed for, what they drew on the walls of their dwellings and carved into rocks they passed on their journeys. It was the very center of their concept of their relationship to the natural world, and it was a cycle that repeated itself on every continent that sustained human life. And in each place, it was a cycle that depended on grass.

These first Americans began their journeys into the center of the continent, following a corridor left by glacial retreats. The land they traveled was a mix of woody plants and grasses, surrounded by denser woodlands. Species of massive mammals shared the continent with them—woolly mammoth, mastodons, giant bears, saber-toothed tigers, and wild ancestors of horses and camels. Using early hunting tools such as deadly slingshots, spears, and the atlatl, a refined, long-distance spear, they slayed these gigantic beasts with great skill and success.

Many small bands of people settled on escarpments and near tributaries and river bottoms, developing farming practices. Others depended almost completely on meat from large grazers, and lived a more nomadic life following the herds. Even those who farmed supplemented their diet with the spoils of massive hunting expeditions into the newly forming grasslands. The first Americans were settling in to their homes.

Around 8,500 years ago, another episode of the continent's up and down climate occurred. It's what modern scientists call the Atlantic-Altithermal Interlude, a period when warming air temperatures caused a further shrinking of the huge glaciers. One of the results was the explosive expansion of grasslands, which spread in a rich swathe over the entire middle third of the continent. Many scientists say that it was also this change in climate that caused the demise of the megafauna—mammoth, mastodon,

sabre-toothed tiger, and nearly sixty other similarly sized species that became extinct at this time. Others contend that the mass extinctions were caused by the weapon-bearing humans, who overhunted their slow, unsuspecting prey, which were unaccustomed to predators as cunning as humans.

Whatever the reason, the result was the same: the megafauna were gone, but smaller mammals remained. The most plentiful and powerful of these mammals was a relative of the megafauna. It was the bison.

The Sacred Land

A man climbs from the cab of a late-model pickup and extends a hand from the pocket of his black leather jacket. "Joe Williams," he says softly as he nods in unison with the gentle squeeze of his hand. Cowboy boots and blue jeans are his garb; aviator glasses tinted against the noontime sun prevent a view of his eyes. The ground beneath him is pebbly with gravel, spread over this small section of prairie to keep the cars and trucks of visitors from digging into the soil. This parking lot is a portal to a very special place just ahead. Joe Williams is a spiritual leader of the Dakota Sioux, and he has traveled from his home on a nearby reservation to talk—a little—about this sacred land.

The land he stands on, in southwestern Minnesota, is now known as the Jeffers Petroglyphs Historic Site, and is managed by the state's historical society. For some, it is a tourist stopover in the middle of an island of virgin prairie, surrounded by fertile farmlands that have faithfully yielded soybeans and corn for more than a hundred years. For Joe Williams and many others, it is a holy place.

What *all* visitors see—unless the snow is so deep as to cover them—are mammoth slabs of Sioux quartz protruding in flat, powerful sheets from the face of the prairie. Reddish and fairly smooth, these half dozen slabs—also called erosional remnants—stretch across a good half mile, and are surrounded by tall stalks of bluestem that encircle the site like sentinels.

What *some* visitors see, especially when the sun is low and angled just right, are the rock carvings of people who hunted these lands for thousands of years. The symbols, which were most likely carved over a span of five thousand years, appear to represent a host of animals and human-like forms, together with ancient tools and hunting weapons, like the *atlatl*, precursor to the bow and arrow. But all told, it is the shaggy, four-legged, hump-backed animal that appears most often. It is the bison.

On this sunny, brisk October afternoon, Joe Williams walks away from the gravelly parking lot into the tall stand of grasses well into their autumn maturity. The big bluestem is waist-high, with seed heads turned red with the cooling temperatures. Wildflowers like blue aster and goldenrod dot the sea of grasses, splashing brilliant color among the waves of gold. Joe settles on the powdery green of a sage plant, picks a sprig, and rubs it between the palms of his hands, cupping them over his nose and breathing deeply. "Calming," he says before moving on.

When Joe is at the petroglyphs, he sees the large slabs of rock, as others do, but he also feels a spiritual connection to the place. For him, these rocks are sacred. He picks up a small, smooth stone from the ground and says that it, too, has a life and place within the universe. He motions across the prairie and says that life-enriching medicines are growing before him. He raises his hands to the sky and says that life-giving energy comes from the sun.

His is a life set in the middle of a time when most people live seventy-miles-per-hour, air-conditioned lives. Joe lives on a reservation, and his life has a different pace, bridging a gap between two worlds. He wears Western clothing and served in the American Armed Forces, but he also spends a great deal of time with the people of his tribe, mending their ills with age-old wisdoms received from *Wakan Tonka*, The Great Spirit. He is at the helm of many spiritual ceremonies, where members of his tribe gather in ages-old rituals, just a stone's throw from the community's new casino. He reveres the ground beneath his feet and the sun above his head, and has spent much of his life learning from an elder who spent much of his life learning from others before him, on and on back to a time when the first of his people walked on this place on earth. And carved these stories in stone.

LEFT: *For Native Americans living on the prairies, everything in the natural world is alive with a vibrant force that is part of the Creator. Grasses, flowers, animals, insects, and fellow people are thus all to be treated with respect.*

RIGHT: *This young woman is identified only as a Sioux maiden. Like other women of her people, she would have spent much of her time preparing bison hides for use as tipi covers or clothing and gathering wild foods and preparing these foods by preserving or cooking them. These lifeways existed largely unchanged for millennia until Europeans arrived in North America.*

FAR RIGHT: *The rhythms of life for Native Americans on the prairie followed the seasons, and some prairie peoples began their calendar with the first snowfall. Each year, or "winter," the people of the tribe would select one important event from that year, and a representation of the event would be painted on a piece of buffalo hide. This "winter count" effectively chronicled the history of the people.*

I have resented that prairie is not an Indian word. It should have been, and sounds as if it might have been. The one thing the Indian came nearer to owning than any other, was prairie.

—Wayne Fields

As these large herbivores thrived on the tender grasses, a below-ground world continued to expand. Beneath the gentle crust of the earth, minerals and nutrients left over from thousands of watery years became the perfect host for species of grasses that collected energy from the sun and sent it deep into the ground, sent it through roots that grew, thrived, and built nutrient-rich material. Like grazers in grasslands around the globe, bison thrived on the grasses, chewing off the tempting tops of the plants, but leaving behind the plant's less appealing base, along with its vast underground storehouse of energy and broadest area of growth—its roots.

Gigantic herds of bison followed the shifts in the protein content of the dominant grasses, which was ultimately determined by the earth's antipodal rotations, intricately connected to the course of the sun whose light bathed the meadows in the warmth of life itself. It was as if the prairie were the lungs of the continent—breathing life in and out, solar energy in and protein out—and the creatures knew when each latitude brought forth the abundance.

LEFT: *The relationship between bison and Native Americans is reflected in ceremonial, spiritual, and practical elements of their societies, and bison were honored in buffalo dances and other rituals.*
BELOW: *The buffalo was a source of great spiritual strength for many of the Plains tribes, including the Cheyenne, Crow, Plains Cree, Pawnee, Kiowa, and Sioux. Here, Cheyenne dancers prepare to join the ceremony.*

RIGHT: *One of the defining differences among tall-, mixed- and shortgrass prairies is average annual rainfall— tallgrass prairie receives the most. Rainfall determined which species of grasses and wild-flowers would thrive in a particular area, and this in turn determined to some extent the animals that would live there. In this view of Kansas tallgrass prairie, an ice storm has coated each blade of grass, creating a shimmering landscape.*

Loneliness, thy other name, thy one true synonym, is prairie.

—W.A. Quayle

The courses of sun and moon controlled the winds. As they played about the skies, the winds hurried the clouds to allow sunlight, and they brought snow or rain—and lightning. If the vast tracts of dense grasses in one area had received sparse rainfall and thus were dry, a single lightning strike would touch off a fire that could burn unchecked for thousands of square miles. But the growing buds of the dominant species of grasses were belowground, and regenerated in only a few days.

The tender new shoots, freed from the cover of years of accumulated dead thatch above them, would spring up. The bison craved these fresh new stands and would search diligently for them—migrating in their millions back and forth across the prairie, year in and year out.

Of all the prairie lands in North America, the tallgrass prairie always received the most rainfall. These grasses were farthest from the Rocky Mountain rainshadow, and they frequently received a flow of moist air from the Gulf of Mexico. Water was one of the keys to the renewal of these long grasses. At eye level, the prairie often could appear somewhat monotonous, but it was not so much broken up as embroidered by the trees that hugged the defiles of the thousands of crucial watersheds, the only place woody plants could survive in this ecosystem shaped by regular fire.

Mixed-grass and shortgrass prairie grew where rainfall was less abundant, so the height of these grasses was often fairly uniform. By contrast, the fabric of the tallgrass prairie was a quilt of huge, shifting patches: some areas recently burned, some recently grazed by bison, and others with mile after mile of grasses almost six feet tall.

FAR LEFT: *Streams and rivers coursing through the tallgrass prairie create small "gallery forests" along the water's edge. Here, Kings Creek, at Konza Prairie near Manhattan, Kansas, provides moisture for a variety of broad-leaf plants and trees.*

LEFT: *Dark, lowering clouds signal rain on the Broken Kettle Grasslands of Iowa.*

BELOW: *A Pawnee family stands in front of their earth-lodge. The Pawnee, along with some other Plains tribes, excavated the floors of their lodges so the dwellings were partially below-ground.*
RIGHT: *A showy yellow evening primrose (Oenothera sp.) blooms at the close of day.*
OPPOSITE: *Thickspike gayfeather and bluestem create a tapestry of purple and russet that stretches as far as the eye can see. Tallgrass prairie once covered more than 250 million acres, but now only remnants of undisturbed tallgrass remain.*

As foretold by their ancestors' existence on other continents, a synergy was created among humans, bison, and grass. Bison ate grass, humans ate bison. And the grass needed the bison, as well. As they moved, the bisons' bodies processed the energy and nutrients they gained from the grasses and deposited back onto the ground what was waste to their systems. Their urine and dung included greatly concentrated nutrients, especially nitrogen, in forms that grasses could readily use. It was a beneficial system, because the nutrient recycling done by the animals was far speedier than the slow decay of plants' detritus.

As ultimate opportunists, humans thrived in this system. In all, some thirty tribes made their homes on or along the forested edges of the North American grasslands. In some parts of the prairies, people settled in semipermanent villages and began to farm the land. Dwellings were often substantial, with post-and-beam construction. Some settled groups lived in grass houses, constructed of a framework of wooden poles covered with grass thatch. Other Plains peoples lived in earthlodges, which consisted of a framework of wooden poles covered with layers of branches, grass, sod, and an outer layer of packed earth. These homes were well

No living man will see again the long-grass prairie, where a sea of prairie flowers lapped at the stirrups of the pioneer. We shall do well to find a forty here and there on which the prairie plants can be kept alive as species. There were a hundred such plants, many of exceptional beauty. Most of them are quite unknown to those who have inherited their domain.

—P. Gruchow

insulated and had a central hearth; smoke escaped through a hole in the roof, which could be covered in bad weather.

Over time, agricultural practices grew to include large fields of beans, squash, sunflowers, pumpkins, and maize. Eventually, these Plains societies were producing nearly 25 bushels of dried corn per acre of land. The planting practice of these early agriculturists was often referred to as "The Three Sisters" system of planting. Using three types of plants in one field—each with different nutrient needs and root depths—these stewards of the land kept the soil healthy. This "polyculture" form of planting mimicked the natural system of native grasses and their co-existing species, such as nitrogen-fixing legumes and a host of wildflowers.

CLOCKWISE FROM NEAR RIGHT: *Wild prairie rose (Rosa arkansana) was well known to Native Americans, who ate its vitamin-C-rich fruits (called hips), cooked its spring shoots, and brewed its young leaves and stems into tea; Indians used rattlesnake master (Eryngium yuccifolium) to heal snakebites, hence its name; a native of North American prairies, blazing star (Liatris spicata) is attractive to butterflies; the cheery daisylike flowers of black-eyed Susan (Rudbeckia hirta) are a familiar midsummer sight; the leaves of catclaw sensitive briar (Schrankia nuttallii) fold closed when touched or in high winds.*

FAR RIGHT: *As the sun sets on the prairie, spring-blooming evening primroses open their lustrous petals.*

These early prairie peoples hunted and gathered their food with the flow of the seasons. Even settled groups often abandoned their villages to follow the herd, thus both settled and nomadic peoples lived at least part of the year in easily transported, hide-covered shelters called tipis. In many of these societies, it was meat that fueled their subsistence—up to six pounds of it per person, per day—so it was the hunt that made the largest impression on their lives. While elk, deer, antelope, turtles, and fish were among the prey, it was the bison that made up the vast majority of their bounty. Hunting skills, therefore, became a central focus of the tribe, as they developed and refined weapons and techniques.

A single herd of bison could number in the tens of thousands, and might stretch five miles wide and twelve miles long. For the hunters, understanding the movements and composition of the herd was crucial. What attracted the bison to a new area? The answer was fresh grass. And the hunters soon realized that fire encouraged the growth of fresh grass. They also understood that the bison congregated in large herds with the

LEFT: *A dramatic wall cloud forms at sundown over the tallgrass. Wall clouds are associated with very strong thunderstorms, and a rotating wall cloud may precede a tornado. Some Native American tribes created prayers or ceremonies devoted to influencing the weather.*

BELOW: *During buffalo hunting time, Plains peoples lived in tipis, which were highly portable. This archival photograph shows a family posed outside their tipi.*

young—those with the preferred tender meat—encircled by the old. The natural cycles of the grass and the habits of the bison informed these Plains peoples' hunting practices. The Native Americans of the prairies set fire to the land to deter encroaching forests and to ensure the tender young shoots of grass the bison so craved. They also set fires to move their prey, often driving them en masse over cliffs to their deaths. With practice, they refined their spear points, arrowheads, and bows, making themselves masters of the hunt.

From the bison, the hunting peoples took nearly everything they needed to survive. Its bounty provided sustenance, shelter, and the materials for tools and weapons. A male bison weighed nearly 2,000 pounds, a female, nearly 1,000 pounds, and nearly every ounce was either consumed for energy or fashioned into something useful.

These rhythms of agrarian or hunting life continued for the Plains Indians for many generations before another major change occurred.

> *As I looked about me I felt the grass was the country, as the water is the sea. The red of the grasses made all the great prairie the color of wine-stains…*
>
> —Willa Cather

An animal once familiar to the North American grasslands returned to its ancestral grounds. After thousands of generations, it was much smaller and refined by domestication. And this time, the animal carried humans on its back….

In 1541 Francisco de Coronado and his entourage launched an expedition to explore the self-proclaimed territory of New Spain in the American Southwest. Coronado ventured north from Mexico almost as far into the center of the continent as the Flint Hills of Kansas, looking for lost cities of gold—a legend he had heard from Native Americans in Mexico. Instead, he found the world's finest grasslands, glowing with gold from the sun. Two of the greatest consequences of Coronado's mission were unintended: first, his expedition traded or lost several horses to the Native Americans—an event that would forever change the culture of the Plains Indians. Secondly, although his expedition's written accounts praised the prairie lands, his failure to find fabulous wealth began the prairie's misleading reputation as The Great American Desert.

So as a result, the expedition equipped the Indians with their most powerful hunting tool—and bought them a little more time on the plains before others of European descent would venture onto their land. The lives of the Native Americans would eventually become intertwined—even willingly at times—with Europeans hungry for land and opportunity.

LEFT: *Autumn is a pleasant time of year on the prairies, with warm days and cool nights. Even before the first frost, grasses change to gold or russet and sumac (Rhus sp.) begins to turn a spectacular red, signalling the coming of winter.*

RIGHT: *Perhaps the most famous photographer of Native Americans, Edward Sheriff Curtis portrayed his subjects in a romantic and stylized way. In many of Curtis's photographs, like this one, titled* The Old Cheyenne *and copyright 1927, it's clear that he is acutely aware of immortalizing the "vanishing American."*

FAR LEFT, TOP: *Though this tribal portrait is labeled "Sioux Tribe," the word Sioux is an abbreviation of nadouessioux, meaning "little snakes," a name given to them by their Chippewa enemies. While the name Sioux has become accepted, the people of the Sioux nation prefer to be known as Dakota, Lakota, or Nakota, according to their language group.*

FAR LEFT, BOTTOM: *A Pawnee woman and her daughter construct the framework for an earthlodge. Girls were expected to help their mothers with tasks like cooking, gathering food, and caring for younger children; in this way, they learned the skills and values of their culture.*

LEFT: *Like most Curtis portraits, this one, called Spotted Bull— Mandan, shows the quiet dignity of the Native American people.*

Of Tipis, Buffalo, and Tornadoes

Native Americans who lived on the eastern edge of the plains, among the tall grasses, farmed the rich bottomlands of the rivers. During the months they were tending their crops, they lived in semipermanent grass dwellings or earthlodges. When it was time for the buffalo hunt, a decision made by a tribe's chiefs and often tied to the height of the corn or other grasses, the Indians would pack up their village, abandoning their lodges for the easily portable tipis.

Dogs, and then horses, were used to haul the tipis. The 12- to 20-foot-long poles of the tipi, usually made straight and smooth by the women, were attached to an animal's shoulder with a harness. Leather straps would bind the household goods and skins to these travois. At the end of a day's travel, the conical tents, about 18 feet in diameter at the base, were quickly assembled, placed so that they would face east. Nineteenth-century observers reported, "The tent covers are made of buffalo skins, scraped so thin as to transmit light. These [tipis] when new are quite white, and a village of them presents a beautiful appearance." Tightly sewn skins were stretched over a pole foundation. Most tipis featured some sort of artwork—perhaps a record of a warrior's deeds or religious symbols. Sides of the tipi could be raised to let breezes in, or shut tight to keep out the elements. In the same fashion, there were flaps at the top which could be manipulated to let air in or smoke out.

All of the semi-nomadic tribes' belongings needed to be lightweight yet durable. Rugged envelopes and sacks made out of rawhide—called *parfleches*—were fashioned to carry sacred bundles and personal belongings, and were strong enough to withstand the jostling of the journey, which could cover hundreds of miles.

Once the chief of a tribe (or several tribes, as many Plains Indians gathered together for the annual hunts) decided on a camping spot, all members would be pressed into service. It was paramount that all be ready for the sacred and life-sustaining hunt. The Native Americans used every part of the buffalo. Flesh and organs provided food; hides were used for clothing, lodging, weaponry, ropes, drums, bull boats, and spiritual ceremonies; bones and horns for utensils, tools, and weapons; organs and fluids for medicines, oils, and grease.

—*Kristin Frizzell*

BELOW: *The tipi is an ingenious solution to an architectural dilemma, making good use of one of prairie's chief available resources: buffalo hides. It is also warm, waterproof, and highly portable.*

Following is a firsthand account by Ely Moore, Jr., of a buffalo hunt with the Miamis in 1854. It tells of the superior skill of the Native Americans in hunting their prey, and also of their ability to read nature's many signs.

Our party was a strong one, able to cope with any of the hostiles on the plains. It consisted of 400 men and 50 squaws of the five tribes; 20 Shawnees and 30 Pottawatomies, all well armed. Our equipment consisted of about 100 wagons, two yoke of oxen to each, and 200 pack-ponies. All these were necessary to transport home our meat and robes.

About three o'clock the next afternoon, when within a few miles of what was to be our permanent camp, we were side-tracked by an immense herd of buffalo on their way south. They were soon encroaching upon the head of our train, so that it became necessary to order out a strong guard to keep then from running over us. Against our will we were forced to camp without water, and were held in that plight until ten o'clock the next day. This herd of buffalo, the Indians insisted, was the largest herd they had ever seen. As far as the eye could reach was one moving mass of buffaloes. To protect our camp from invasion the guard killed thirty or more of the shaggy fellows that night. As good grass was near by our temporary camp, they soon came to a long feeding halt, and exhibited no fear as we passed by them to our permanent camp.

Our chief was something of a military man, and our train moved with the precision of a well-drilled command of soldiers. When within a half mile of camp an order would be given to the squaws, and instantly all would dismount, each having been provided with a gunny-sack, and commence collecting dry buffalo chips with which to cook our meals. Then fifty young bucks would slide from their ponies, and with an ax and short-handled spade begin digging fire-pits. Each driver would then place his wagon in position, which, when all in, would form a perfect circle within which we all camped. A detail would then be ordered for culinary purposes, one for water-carriers, another for herders and guard duty.

The morning after reaching our permanent camp a hundred of us were ordered to commence killing, as thousands of buffalo were feeding near by. In an hour the killing, skinning, tanning of robes, and jerking and preserving of meat was in full operation.

The killing is where the fun and danger comes in. The buffaloes soon took the alarm and started south. Thousands of them, however, were loath to leave the good grass, and, breaking from the main herd, commenced to circle about a mile from us. This was what we most desired, for the nearer camp they fell the better.

The Indian plan of killing is vastly different from that adopted by the white man, for the reason that when on the march the buffalo bulls invariably line the outside of the herd, with their heads down and outward, thus guarding the cows and calves from all enemies. The white hunter, disregarding this gallantry on the part of the bulls, would almost always kill the nearest thing in sight, and after the hunt would be in possession of bulls, and bulls only, whose hide, texture of meat, and flavor is questionable.

The Indians' plan is this: As they approach the herd, always keeping pace with the buffaloes, they shoot down several bulls, and as a gap in the line is thus made they dash their ponies through the breach, conforming speed and direction with that of the herd, gradually working toward the center, where they find the cows, calves, and two-year-olds, thus securing the finest robes and choicest meats. When their revolvers are empty, for only revolvers or bows and arrows can be safely used in this mode of killing, they gradually worm themselves out of the herd in the same manner as they had entered.

The great danger in this style of killing the buffalo is from a wounded bull, a timid horse, or a dog hole. However, we only had one man wounded and one pony killed during our hunt. Jimmie Squirrel, a Miami Indian, had the calf of his leg torn loose by the thrust of a wounded bull, the same blow disemboweling his horse. This was caused by his pony sinking his leg in a dog hole and so being unable to speedily recover his footing.

As stated, this mode of killing is coupled with some danger; but did you ever know of a real sport that was not? The risk but added spice to the hunt. It braced the nerves and caused the blood to ebb and flow with the speed and force of a trip-hammer. Imagine yourself shooting your way into a herd of buffaloes numbering thousands upon thousands, with their red glaring eyes and polished wicked horns menacing you at every step, your horse guided solely by the sway of your body to the right, or left, alert to the spur, and obedient to the command "sle," slow, or "hi-o," halt, that you may the more accurately place the lead a little below and back of the shoulder-blade. Imagine yourself, I say, placed in this condition with three or four hundred shouting and shooting Indians bestride their nimble ponies, and bringing to the ground at almost every shot this noble but dangerous game, and then assert that it is not sport superb, far excelling all sports of the present day.

We killed more than a hundred buffalo in our first day's hunt, as the counting of tongues told us that night. The tongues are cut from all the buffaloes that are killed, and then carefully dried, as they are delicious eating and serve also as a "tally-sheet," for upon reaching home they are counted, thus giving the exact number of animals killed.

During six weeks of hunting we moved our camp but once, and then for only a few miles, as buffaloes were constantly around us and water abundant in what the Indians called "Blind River." By digging two or three feet through a crust of sand we came to running water, which was both sweet and cool.

There is an enormous amount of work attached to such a camp and hunt, especially as we killed 1700 buffaloes (the number of tongues we had upon reaching home). All these animals had to be skinned, robes dried and tanned, and the hams cut into pieces similar to the smoked beef of the present day. The rest of the animal not eaten by the party was subjected to the "jerking" process—that is, pulled off the carcass in thin strips and dried; and when so properly dried it would keep for years. We generally had no blue-bottle flies on the plains in those days after August. The air was so pure that meat would cure in a few days.

One morning during the third week of our hunt it was extremely sultry and warm—so sultry that breathing was an effort—but soon after breakfast we started for an immense herd of buffaloes feeding near our camp. Upon reaching the herd I felt a want of enthusiasm in the sport before me, and noticed the same lack of vim in all the Indians as well as in our horses.

About noon, just as the enthusiasm of our sport began to assert itself, the signal to return to camp was given—a flag raised form the chief's tent, and three shots at short intervals. We promptly obeyed the summons, marveling much why the order. On the way to camp we noticed the wagons en route to the field over which we hunted for the purpose of gathering up meat and robes, all returning to camp. I at once sought the reason for the order and the hurry and bustle that was noticeable on all sides. The chief, in answer to my inquiry, pointed to the sun, and then I noticed millions of insects, grasshoppers, winging their way east. So dense were they that the sun was obscured for minutes at a time. The chief, with gestures of foreboding evil, further explained: "They (grasshoppers) know. Devil wind come, kill all, may be. Great Spirit knows best!"

Many of us were put to work with ax and spade to sink our wagons, cutting a trench three feet in length, six inches wide and two feet deep. The wheels of our wagons were then placed in these trenches to more securely hold them against a heavy wind. The ponies were brought within the enclosure, the corral formed by the wagons. The cattle were herded close to our camp, and a double guard stationed around them to prevent a possible stampede. Then the wagon-covers were tied down with ropes of buffalo hides cut in narrow strips and tied together; all the hunting horses were ordered within the corral, and other preparations made for safety.

It was after five o'clock when all this was accomplished, and at that time could be seen in the southwest a dark, greenish-purple cloud-shaped lowering monster that had many laterals that were licking up the beasts, earth, water, and air to satiate the ponderous maw of this fiend of might. Respiration was a struggle, the utter stillness most enervating, and the darkness impenetrable. Our awed cattle, with bewailing moans, lolling tongues, and nervous lifting and stamping of feet, were pitiable to see. The fear-shaken ponies stood huddled together, as if for mutual protection, with the head of one thrown over the neck of another, or with their heads close to the ground. Our head chief, mounted, occupied the center of the encampment. The squaws sought shelter in the empty wagons, and the hunters with their arms around their horses' necks—for the Indian loves his horse—stood and awaited the result.

Just then a sound as of muffled drums reached us, and, as a rift in the clouds shot a glare of light upon the camp, I stole a hasty look around me. There stood the Indians, stolid, but in an attitude of supplication to the Great Spirit. Now the storm came on apace, descending with unmitigated violence upon the quaking, dusky forms, who seemed awaiting their doom.

We were literally cover-wrapped in an electric cloud. As electric sparks snapped from the tips of our horses' ears, the moaning, shivering creatures pressed close to their masters. The wheels of our wagons were circled by the electric fluid, and many bolts were drawn from our wagon-beds. Then came the wind, and with it hail of irregular shape and great size, descending with such force that many of our cattle had their eyes forced out of their sockets, and many of our ponies were badly lacerated on the back and flank, while some of our wagon-covers were tattered and torn into strips. At that time the cyclone proper appeared egg-shaped, and its points north and east were a mile or more in length. As it neared us it seemed to bound into the air some hundreds of feet. Just as one of the drag-nets or feeders of the parent dragon reached our encampment it was apparently struck by lightning, or was surcharged, for a downpour of sand, earth, grass, weeds, and limbs of trees was deposited within our corral of wagons, amounting to many hundred tons. The breaking of this drag-net is all that saved us. The force was broken, and satiated its gluttonous intent by destroying a few wagons and filching some bales of robes.

After the destroying fiend passed over we gave thanks, and had a jolly supper. And what a transition! The faces that a short time before were blanched with fear and despair now wore smiles, and all joined in jests

The next morning was clear and cool, and after much labor in removing the debris deposited by the storm we went to work repairing damages. There was no game in sight, nor did any appear until the following morning.

The reader of the present day must not suppose that we wantonly killed the noble game. No party of hunters was ever more economical of the herd than we. Besides, we always followed up and killed the wounded animals—a service foreign to the idea of the white hunters—thus preventing their starving or being tormented and finally eaten by the wolves.

Do you realize at that time the buffalo belonged to the Indians? So they believed. They looked upon them as their herds of cattle.

Judging from the number of buffaloes I saw during our hunt, I did not believe the united armies of the world could exterminate them in many years.

On our way home, and but a few miles from our deserted camp, we saw where the cyclone that jumped us had stripped acres of sod and soil from the prairies. We also found two dead buffaloes completely denuded of hair, and every bone in their bodies crushed. These animals must have been picked up by the cyclone, carried to a great height, and then dashed to the earth.

BELOW: *Native Americans danced for many reasons, including to honor animals and to pray for good hunting. Though some dances could be attended by out-siders, others were deeply sacred, for the tribe alone.*

RIGHT: *As settlers took over the prairies, relations with Native Americans grew increasingly strained, though some white men were trusted. Here, former Indian Agent William Bent poses with Southern Arapaho leader Little Raven and his children.*

With the speed and hauling capacities provided by the horse, the Plains Indians prospered. They organized elaborate seasonal hunting par-ties, during which the men of the tribe left their permanent villages on the fringes of the grass for weeks on end and followed the herds into the grasses. When they returned, their travois would be filled with the spoils of the hunt; sometimes the number of bison killed in a single expedition reached into the thousands.

The women in the tribe assumed the responsibilities of transform-ing the carcasses into a winter's living. Every bit of the bison was used. Meat was dried and stored for winter. The fur was made into robes, and the skins were tanned for hides that could be sewn into clothing or cover-ings for tipis. Bones were fashioned into farming implements and other tools, the tallow was stored for a variety of cooking uses. While the new hunting prowess brought an increased workload for the women of the tribes, it brought extra free time for the men of these gender-divided com-munities—time to develop further their art and spiritual ceremony.

Plains Indian societies developed complex religious observances that, at their core, provided the spiritual energy for the renewal of the natural world and the recognition of the place of human beings within it. The seasonal cycle and the dominant place of bison within their lives are well evidenced in the Plains Indians' ceremonies and rituals. Diversity of spiri-tual pursuits gave way to a common desire for supernatural sanction for bountiful harvest of planted crops and teeming herds of bison. Religious inquiry and study also provided the means to place the natural environ-ment in a meaningful order and conveyed a moral code through which humans, animals, and plants were respectively nurtured and exploited.

And so it was, thousands of years after their arrival on the conti-nent, that humans were at the top of the food chain, firmly established as the dominant species. Their only significant enemies were disease, inter-tribal warfare, famine, flood, and other acts of nature. Over time, each would occur in varying degrees, but it would be the white-skinned others of their species who would ultimately upset the system. And it would happen, in the annals of the continent, in a relative blink of an eye.

The Indian Removal

As waves of settlers moved across the country, planting crops and establishing homes, the original inhabitants of the land were themselves uprooted. First the eastern tribes, and then their counterparts in the plains region, were displaced as America pursued its Manifest Destiny. In 1825, the US government officially created the Indian Territory for all of the country's native peoples, including in the territory land allotted for permanent reservations and land already occupied by the Plains Indians. Almost immediately, however, the Plains tribes were pressured to cede their land to the government in exchange for "unalterable rights" to a greatly reduced territory.

The devastating effects of this removal and the increasing reduction of territory is well documented in history. Many people in the northeastern and southeastern tribes died during their arduous enforced march to the Indian Territory, and the survivors were placed in a geographical area and circumstance completely alien to them. The Plains Indians who accepted the government's offers of smaller lands soon found themselves ill-equipped to deal with the very government that claimed to protect them—a government that was concurrently extending rights for those same lands to railroad companies and goldrushers, while turning a blind eye to settlers who were illegally homesteading on Indian lands.

The might of the US Army and the sheer numbers of the settlers moving into the region were no match for those Native Americans who resisted moving to the reservations. After some final battles in the late 1800s, including Wounded Knee in December 1890, the last of the Plains Indians were removed to reservations. The men and women who had lived their lives following the rhythms of the seasons and the bison now wrestled with finding new identities. Men were no longer warriors in the traditional sense. Without the bison, there was no need for their hunting skills, no need for the rituals and ceremonies that accompanied the hunts. There were no longer raids to prepare for, and even some dances and ceremonies were circumscribed by the government. There were no buffalo hides for the women to tan, no meat to prepare and preserve. Kiowa Chief Curly Head reflected on a life lived with one foot in each world in a speech presented at the University of Oklahoma at the turn of the century.

I am glad to see the young men and women here. I want to see more Indian boys and girls take advantage and get a good education and go back home and help the older Indians such as I am. I look to the younger generation for salvation and help for the remaining days I may have with my people.

You people know that at one time we owned all this land and territory, but by your superiority you overcame and took away all we had. For this reason I want you, when you seen an Indian, to respect him as a citizen. Ask everybody in the country, state or anywhere who has any kind of influence to use that influence so that the American Indian will be benefited.

We have no written history. I am seventy-nine or eighty years old and our traditions and stories are handed down.... When I became a man, began to think like a man, I remember very clearly when there were droves of buffalo on the plains. There were plenty in olden days. As a boy, when the old Indians would make their chase and the calves were turned out, the Indian boys would kill the calves. I was a healthy boy and healthy more because I would eat the kidneys of calves and drink the blood of calves. Very seldom heard of a person dying young. The Great Spirit gave us the buffalo and you have also heard of the deer. Women folks would come and dress the meat and take it home to the family and everyone would have plenty.

After the Medicine Lodge Treaty, I enlisted as a scout at Ft. Sill. After the Medicine Lodge Treaty, there was a boundary line made by the Kiowa-Apaches which was not accepted by a greater part of the Indians. Rather than be put on a reservation, a great part of the tribes left and went into Mexico. The scouts followed them to see if they could not bring back the Indians, and it was on this trip that I saw something that made my heart cry....

We saw several wagons scattered over the hilltop—five men to each wagon. The men were clothed in buffalo hides with the hair still on it. They wore glasses with powerful guns and they were shooting the buffaloes. In olden days, he [the Indian] knew the Great Spirit was watching his tribe. It gave him plenty. The lakes and streams were full of things to eat, the prairies were full of things to eat. Money was no necessity then. I was a happy man, and I think I was better off then. When the Anglo-Saxon race came, they tried to change me and I am now a poor man. I have lost all that I love. Hardship is taking hold of the Indian race. In olden times, I could go out as far in the open as I please. I could go where I wanted to and when I pleased, but since the white man has placed me on the reservation with white people surrounding me, I am no more a happy man.

Every time I come here I always hope and pray and wish that since we have to be adopting white man's civilization some, our only hope is education and I hope that in the future years that my children, our boys and girls, will take advantage of all the present day education and civilization that they may be able to compete with their white brothers. That is my hope, wish and prayer when I visit this institution.

CHAPTER THREE

the plains and the plow

By the time French explorers, trappers, and missionaries entered the prairie from the north in the early 1700s, traveling the rivers south from the Great Lakes in search of lucrative furs for Europe and souls for Christ, the Plains Indians had mastered Coronado's serendipitous gift of the horse. They added this new tool to their clever use of fire in order to greatly increase their annual harvest of bison. Indian populations grew accordingly.

The fur trade was so essential to the French that they aimed to connect with the Spanish colonies; Santa Fe was nearest, so they struck out from the Missouri river overland toward the southwest, unknowingly bypassing the most fertile grasslands. What Louis de Bourgmont, a French explorer of the early eighteenth century, and a few others did see of the tallgrass, they liked, for they dubbed it "prairie"—the French word for meadow. But most of these accounts were from the shortgrass prairies and the desert Southwest, so the moniker "Great American Desert" continued to stick to the entire middle of the continent.

LEFT: *Eighteenth-century French explorers—who had no experience of a landscape like the North American grasslands—called it by the nearest name they knew: "prairie," meaning meadow.*
ABOVE: *More than a century would pass before Europeans would begin to call the prairies their home and plow the fertile pastures.*

Dependent largely on waterborne transportation, the main French and English colonies on the East Coast and in the Great Lakes region had been settled initially by adventurers, ne'er-do-wells, seekers of religious or political freedom, or others who did not fit into the stratified socio-economic structure of the Old World. They had watched their more privileged countrymen—whether with inherited social standing or the simple advantage of being first in birth order—continue to control large tracts of Europe's land.

Encouraged by tales of plenty, landless poor and disenfranchised second sons came to the New World in increasing numbers. As the arable land in the original American colonies was snatched up, the next generations pushed westward across the Allegheny Mountains and through the Cumberland Gap. In 1803, the new United States purchased from France most of the land west of the Mississippi River. President Thomas Jefferson sent an expedition, headed by Meriwether Lewis and William Clark, to explore the vast, new territories. Their accounts of huge numbers of game in the tallgrass and mixed-grass prairies sounded good to hunters, but not necessarily to homesteaders. The homesteaders had discovered that the tallgrass prairie, in what they then called the Northwest (parts of what are now Ohio and Indiana and all of Illinois), was breathtakingly fertile. The native prairie grasses had diligently, for thousands of years, taken in both sunlight and airborne carbon. Grazed by the bison and frequently burned by fire, the grasses had prospered, expanded, and sent their deep root systems into the fecund soil. Illinois was almost completely prairie, and was almost entirely given over to the plow by the 1850s, even as it was being dubbed "The Prairie State."

In the late 1840s, the Mexican War and the California Gold Rush, as well as improvements in overland wagon travel, prompted a few bands of mountain men, notably Jim Bridger, Bill Sublette, and Kit Carson, to blaze wagon train routes to the West: the Santa Fe, California, and

The Promise of the Prairie

Pennsylvania-born adventurer Abbie Bright joined her older brother Philip in Kansas in 1871. She was twenty-one years old. Excerpts from her diary show the both hardships and the joys of life on the prairie.

April 18th...*Brother Philip...says if I want to come west, I can take up Government Land, and after living on it six months, can prove up on it by paying $1¼ an acre for it. He took up a claim some time ago, and if I go— I can stay with him, his house is almost finished. I am only to take heavy strong clothing and what ever I will for a bed....I wonder what mother will say, when she hears I am going to Kansas....*

May 2...*This is a new settlement. A year ago I under stood there were no white women within 15 or 20 miles. Now there are several families scattered along the River. Last winter the Osage Indians camped along the river. Their tepees are still standing, I have been told.*

[May] 8th...*This is the Osage Preemption Land, or The Osage Trust Lands. You select a claim of 160 acres, then you "file on it." After living on it six months, and doing a certain amount of improve ments, you pay $1.25 an acre, and then it is yours.*

Philip has been on his claim that long, has broke some land, and planted corn. He and some men have selected my claim, and when he goes to W[ichita] he will "file on it." Then no one can file on the same land.

He selected a suitable place, and plowed it for a garden, not having a harrow, he hitched the oxen to big brush and dragged it back and forth until it was well raked....I have no hoe yet, but with the help of a stick, I have managed to plant a number of seeds....

[May] 29th *Keeping house at last; moved last week. The cabin is back from the river, with big cottonwoods trees in front. The wind in the tree tops keep up a constant sing-song. The cabin is 12 by 12 feet, with a fire place made of sticks daubed with mud. The roof is split limbs covered with dirt, and now there is a growth of sunflowers and grass on it....*

ABOVE: Some of the most accurate accounts of life on the prairie were penned by candlelight in diaries like those of young Abbie Bright, pictured here.

[May] 31st *Mrs. N moved to town. She gave me her cat. Cats are very scarce here....I am kept busy, sewing for Philip, caring for the garden, and cooking. The baking is tedious, can only bake one loaf at a time in the dutch oven. I knead a loaf out, when that is light, I put it in the oven, and knead out another, and when the first one is baked, the second goes in the oven, and third is kneaded out. All the time I must keep the oven hot enough to bake and brown the bread, which is quite a task and takes three hours or more....*

June 2nd *We have a table now...Supper is ready. For supper we have buffalo, gravy, onions, radishes, molasses, bread, coffee. I was to the garden. It is so far away, and some places I wade through grass almost up to my shoulders.*

June 12 *This is the third week I am housekeeping, and in that time there has been but one women here besides myself. No church, no parties, a wild Indian sort of a life. Plenty of time to commune uninterrupted with Nature, and Nature's god.*

I like it, but if some one said I must stay here always, then I fear I would not....

[July] 4th *The glorious fourth, not a cloud in the sky. Mr. Smith came for me with a two horse wagon, and we took other women along on the way. There were two dozen there counting the children. Five or six bachelors, I was the only single woman—the rest married folks and children.*

Of course, they tease me. They think I am an old maid, 22 and not married. Girls marry so young out here....Then we had canned fruit, lemonade, coffee, and roast meats. A swing for the children, gay conversation for the elders....

July 19...*After breakfast, I called at Springers, and [Mrs. Merkle] went with me to Lanes. Found Mrs. L—in bed shaking with ague. Left Mrs. S there and went on home. It was almost sun down. I was in the middle of the river on a sand bar—dress up—shoes in hand, when I stopped and looked around. The river made a turn, and the trees seemed to meet over the water. It seemed like a lake. On one side a high bank—the trees coming to the waters edge on the other. O, it was beautiful. Think I will never forget the scene.*

[August] 16th *Moved at last. All I remember of the moving, was sitting in the wagon, holding the cat. When we got here, the fever had me, and I could not do a thing. Philip made a bed on the floor, and I laid down. My bed was not fixed yet. When evening came, I was better but scarcely able to walk. ...*

Monday I managed to bake, and Philip fixed things around the house, at 11 had to lie down with chill, and in the p.m. I had to do the same. I had taken quinine but not enough. My fever was over by sun down, but his kept up all night. Yesterday a.m. it left for a short time, then came back, and he was delirious. When I cooled his head with wet towels, the tears would fall. I was in trouble....

[Aug.] 17th *Did not need to lie down all day. It is 4 p.m. have just one hour to write. Brother is still poorly, has fever sometimes, and don't know what he says. My appetite is coming back. These are our dark days, but I am not homesick....*

[Aug.] 18th *Last night he was wild with fever. I cannot write what I suffered. Today he is quite sane, but so weak. Washed this a.m. and baking now....*

[Aug] 21st *I call this place Cottonwood Rest. I want to describe it, if I can. So if I read this journal in years to come, I can then shut my eyes, and know just how it looks now.*

We are about a mile from the river....From here to the river it is very level, and my garden is on this level meadow not far from the dugout. Back of us is prairie a little rolling. The men first dug a well, and at 6 or 7 feet found plenty of water. They covered it, and it is reasonably cool. Not far from the well they dug a trench like walk into the bank, when the sides were 4 ft. high a 12 by 14 ft. hole was dug out, logs laid to fit the sides. When high enough—a big log was laid across the middle the long way, then split limbs and brush were fit on top for a roof, and that was covered with dirt piled on and pressed down. A fire place, and chimney were dug out and built up, at one end, plastered with mud and it answered well.

This room is a little larger than the cabin. My bed in the corner has one leg. A limb with a crotch at one end, is sharpened at the other end, and driven into the ground, 6 feet from one wall and 2 1/2 feet from the other. A pole is laid in the crotch-with one end driven into the ground wall. This supports poles the ends of which are driven in the ground wall at the head of m bed. Then comes my hay filled tick, and my bed is a couch of comfort....

Boxes are nailed to the wall, in which the table furniture is kept, also some groceries. Our chairs are pieces of logs.

Oct. 14th *Over a week since I wrote in my journal. I should have taken it along. Now I have much to write, and most likely will miss some things of interest.*

Saturday I was fixing a duck for dinner, and a goose for Sunday, Jannette Rose came with a letter for me. Father sent me a draft of $300.00 to prove upon my claim.

Then Mr. Springer came for me, they were ready to start on a hunt...I would rather have stayed home, but had promised Mrs. S I would stay with the children. They had the wagon packed, and left soon after we got there. When leaving Mrs. S said, "There is nothing in the house but flour and bacon." I thought she was joking...I was as glad as the children, when they came Wed. evening!

They had to go far, before they found any buffalo, is what had kept them so long. I wanted to go home at once—but they said it was too late, and they were tired, would take me home in the morning. Thursday early—we saw smoke and thought the fire was coming over the divide towards us. So they rushed out to plow a fire guard beyond their hay stacks. The wind favored them, and the fire did not get on their side of the branch....

I was so anxious about my brother—but could not go to him....

Then the boy and I finally got started in the big wagon toward home, and when we rounded the branch we were on burned over ground....Rounding the head of the other branch between the Hall and home, we saw three deer, running toward the sand hills. What a dreary sight it was—not a green thing in sight, except the trees at the river. I had expected to find things looking bad, but my imagination was short, far short of the fact. The prairie had burned black and even; but over the bottom were the grass grew rank, it left the blackened stalks standing. The ground was still hot, and a high wind blowing.

We were both glad to be together again, and I was so relieved to find him as well as he was.

It was cloudy and windy...and I got chilled through. After going to bed fever came on.

Some time later Brother called me. He said if I felt able, I should wrap up well, and come out and see the fire, that it was not likely I would ever see the like again.

The scene was grand beyond description. To the North and within 1/2 mile there was a sheet of flames extending east and west. To the west there was fire beyond fire. Acrost the river, a hay stack was burning. Jake had the logs for his house ready to put up, the fire got among them, and did much damage. I can't give a description of the wild, fearful—yet fascinating sight.

[Oct.] 31st *The last of the month and my time is up. As soon as the plowing is done we will go to [the land office at] Augusta and prove up. It is cold and stormy. Yesterday it rained all day.*

RIGHT: *The Homestead Act was intended to attract settlers to the prairie, and they took up the government's offer in great numbers. But many did not understand the harsh conditions of life on the prairie. Their first task was to build a home on the windy and tree-less land; by neces-sity, they made bricks of the prairie loam, and sodhouses became the norm.*

Oregon Trails. These all crossed large swathes of the prairie, but most of the pioneers who traveled them were headed for the shores of the Pacific Ocean. They were not interested in the productivity of the grasslands. They accepted explorer Zebulon Pike's estimation, blown out of proportion by the popular author Washington Irving, that the Indian territory in Kansas, Nebraska, and Oklahoma was a wasteland.

At the century's midpoint, great forces were powering the nation toward a crisis. Issues of slavery and states' rights that had divided the country for decades had placed the recently plowed tallgrass prairie states—Ohio, Indiana, Michigan, Minnesota, Illinois, and Iowa—in the political division known as the North. Missouri was a "border" state, while Arkansas and Texas were part of the Confederacy; Oklahoma, Kansas, Nebraska, and the Dakotas had not established statehood and therefore remained only territories. The majority of the country's southeastern states had different soils, and therefore a different economy—and a very different culture, one based primarily on slave labor. By 1854, the prizes of Kansas and Nebraska were front and center on the political trading block in Washington, D.C.

The South assumed that Nebraska would gain statehood as a free state and Kansas as a slave state—after all, it was adjacent to Missouri,

Every time I gazed across the prairie it looked like the same old place to me…All I could see was the sky and straw-colored grass…and a few trees about every million miles.

—Lucy Johnson

which held many African-Americans in slavery. The North assumed just the opposite, and was willing to flood the territory with settlers who would vote against slavery.

The Homestead Act of 1854 offered 160 acres free of charge to anyone who could prove he or she was working it. The companion Kansas-Nebraska Act allowed the settlers in each territory to decide the slavery issue. Southerners were leery of placing their most precious economic asset, their slaves, at risk, so few ventured into Kansas. On the other hand, with swing votes to be had, the New England Emigrant Aid Society paid the way of thousands of abolitionist pioneers to Kansas, banking that their reward would be anti-slavery votes. A ferocious border war immediately broke out, contributing to tensions that erupted in the War between the States.

ABOVE: *The prairie lands of Kansas and Nebraska were heavily politicized during the Civil War, but after the war a number of African-Americans saw opportunity in the farmland being given away. Jerry Shores and his family were among the former slaves who settled in Nebraska; his brother settled an adjacent claim.*

Making a Home

Pioneers settled near the prairie's rivers and creeks first, giving them easy access to both water and the trees that grew along the banks. These early settlers' homes were log cabins, and were generally one room that measured about twelve by sixteen feet. Cottonwoods, the trees that seemed to grow along every creek in a tallgrass prairie, were used to build many houses. While plentiful, they were not ideally suited for planks because of their relatively short and crooked limbs. Settlers wrote of the warped shingles and boards they'd crafted out of these trees. Homesteaders would fill gaps and crevices with twigs, rags, and paper, and plaster over the patches with mud or clay.

Early settler Susanna Weymouth remembers her first log cabin home:

When snow fell it always stood as deep in the house as on the ground outside. I have lain in bed with baby, while my husband shoveled the snow out of the room. The big house, being built in June, and the lumber green, by winter time it had become well seasoned, leaving wide cracks an inch or more between each board of the siding. The roof was nearly as well ventilated. I had pasted every scrap of paper I could find over these cracks, and had stuffed in the few rags I could collect also to keep out the cold, but to little purpose.

BELOW: *Building a sodhouse up against a hill meant that only three walls had to be constructed, and the house was a bit more sheltered from the wind. The Rawding family, below, found just such an auspicious spot for their home.*

As the land was settled, even the cottonwoods became scarce as pioneers moved further out onto the prairies. Now, the land itself became building material. Here, homes were carved out of the sides of the hills or crafted out of the thick prairie sod. In these letters to her fiance, Emily Combes, a young woman who went west with her father, wrote about setting up housekeeping in a sodhouse.

On the Prairie
Sun. evening, Jun 18, 1871

My loved one:
Truly, I am "the belle of the county" for I am the only unmarried woman of the eight in the valley....

We selected the site for our house in a sort of horseshoe bend formed by the creek just off the old Topeka and Santa Fe Trail. [Here] the men built a temporary shed, or lean to, by placing a scantling across between the tops of two trees, about ten feet high, then placed boards slanting from the scantling to the ground. Under the shelter we moved our boxes and trunks, using a box for a table. Father brought the cute little cook stove and placed that at one end of the lean to.

Here I cooked the remainder of the week for ten men who were building our house. At night I slept in a cot under the shed while Father slept under the trees. I must admit these are rather unusual conditions for housekeeping. We have no milk, no eggs, no chickens to lay them, no vegetable, no garden, no anything but the trunks of a boarding school girl containing bed linen, clothes, and books. Father's chest of medicine and boxes, a wagon load of lumber, two horses, two harrows and a plow! We have three plates, three cups and saucers. With the stove, fortunately, came an abundance of tin ware and cooking utensils...

It was interesting to watch men build a house of comparatively nothing. They first marked the size of the house 20 x 14, making two rooms—one 12 x 14, the other 8 x 14. Then they dug about a foot and a half into the ground. After the ground was dug sufficiently deep, they laid pieces of sod cut into brick a foot wide and a foot and a half long, eight inches thick and then thoroughly sun baked. They were placed one above the other as real bricks are laid, making walls two feet thick and eight feet high. Frames for the two doors and three windows were put in.

Prairie Home
Sunday, Aug. 27, 1871

Dearest,
[Our house] has a little garden patch at one side where are growing rows of beans and sweet corn. The low creek, gurgling by, with its high banks bordered with scrub cottonwood trees around and behind the house forms a sort of protection. The little sod house, with its little square window is nearly covered with vines.

When we first moved into the house the mice stole Father's pumpkin seeds and he grieved long over their loss. Suddenly pumpkin vines began to appear on top of the sod roof, and their broad leaves and vines completely cover it, hanging down over the door quite artistically. I never before saw such beauty in a pumpkin vine—the huge yellow blooms look like golden trumpets.

The floor of the house is dirt but as dry and hard as cement. We have sprinkled it with water and pounded it with a maul so as to make it hard and smooth as possible. On it are rugs made of coffee sacks and a mat or two of plaited grass. I hope soon to have buffalo robes for rugs.

We have beds of Father's manufacture; a bureau made by the same firm, Dr. Combes, made from a packing box with shelves, curtained with unbleached muslin; a washstand made the same way; another box has an added attraction beside the shelves, a door made by stretching cheese cloth tightly over a frame, hung by leather hinges of buffalo hide. The flour barrel has a square pie board for a top and glories on a cover which makes it look like a small table. I found some nice wide mouthed bottled and two mortars among Father's medicine things and they answer many problems—the bottles especially—one for a rolling pin, another for a churn, two especially large ones for tureen and pitcher.

All around our sod house is the waving grass. Toward the West is the lake with wild ducks, flying, outlined clear against the setting sun. A quail whistles "bob white" and the crickets are chirping. Here by the window in one corner of our dugout is a sort of echo to bob white's lonely call and I do want to see you and my old Ohio home!

Your Em

The partition between the two rooms is also of sod with a doorway between where we will hang a portier made of an Indian blanket. We are very fortunate indeed as we have a board roof over one room. This gives us the benefit of rain water as the water here is very hard. The other room has a thatched roof, boughs of trees covered with sod. Even with plenty of money one could not find other material for a house in this region as lumber must be hauled forty-five miles and is exorbitantly high. These one-storied, sod houses, although they are not prepossessing in appearance, are cool in summer, warm in winter…All my love, Em

ABOVE: This reconstructed sodhouse stands at Toadstool Park in Oglala National Grassland, Nebraska.

After the war, Kansas and Missouri once again became the jumping-off place for the westward migration of European-Americans. It was only four years after General Lee's surrender at Appomattox that the Missouri River was spanned at Kansas City and the final stake was driven in the transcontinental railway in Utah. Now, huge groups of immigrants could not only approach the grasslands by rivers, but could then ride the rails right into the center of the Kansas–Nebraska territories. There they joined together in large numbers to set sail across the inland sea of grass in their "prairie schooners," covered wagons filled with the barest of essentials. Others used the railroads as platforms for the slaughter of millions of head of bison, killed for their hides…and perhaps to deprive the Native Americans of their food source.

Peoples from all over the United States and Europe heard of this free land—once again the grasses were calling. Many immigrants from Northern Europe had even come to America to join the Union army because they had been promised free land on the prairie. Now those who had survived the war signed up by the thousands to reap their reward.

If we never arrived anywhere, it did not matter. Between that earth and that sky I felt erased, blotted out. I did not say my prayers that night: here, I felt, what would be would be.

—Willa Cather

FAR LEFT: *Minnesota's Hole-in-the-Mountain Prairie is now a preserve.*
ABOVE: *A family poses beside their prairie schooner, a farm wagon with a white canvas top.*
LEFT: *The Chrisman sisters took advantage of homesteading laws, each holding three claims and living on them in turn.*

The Threat of Fire

Today, grassland fires are set intentionally to clean the prairie and stimulate growth. They are carefully timed for when wind conditions are just right.

For early settlers, fires were usually not planned but were set by lightning, so "fire" was a word that grabbed the attention of any homesteader. Months of toil could be turned to ash in a matter of moments. A fire's speed depended on the wind and the height of the grasses—factors a homesteader had no control over. His best bet was to plow a row of sod to serve as a firebreak around his property. Pioneers George Hildt and Wallace Wood write in their diaries of one such fire storm.

Reminiscences of Wallace Wood, born in 1855

The grass in the Cottonwood Valley would grow as high as a horse. After the frost in the fall, we were always in danger of a fire. The tall dry grass would make a fire which could travel faster than a man could run. We would make backfires by mowing a stretch around our buildings and then burning the piles of grass. Hardly a year would pass that the fire would not break loose somewhere and come across the hills. If not set by any other means, the lightning would often ignite it…. Sometimes the fire would start down in the Indian Territory of Oklahoma and would be days getting here. Night after night we would see its glow in the distance.

Diary of George Hildt, 1857

Sunday Nov 1 *The prairie on fire all around us & no one but Elick & myself at home. It was a magnificent sight and had been, I thought, well represented in paintings that I had seen. But there was some difference to look at the real thing itself coming towards 50 tons of hay worth $20 dollars a ton on the ground or $30 at Kansas City. As we had taken the precaution to plow a few furrows away from the stacks we did not feel as uneasy as we otherwise should. But nevertheless the raging flame at every side excited us, & tonight as I am writing the horizon is lighted up at every side as if we were surrounded with furnaces and all of them were burning ore. We had been uneasy for some time about our large amount of hay at risk but now I shall sleep soundly as the prairie is burned all around them and in some directions for 10 miles beyond & they are safe.*

RIGHT: *While the delicate frost-covered grasses at this restored Illinois prairie are undeniably beautiful, winter was a dangerous time as well. Many European settlers arrived on the prairie with experience in harsh climates, but they were often unprepared for the journey itself—ten thousand individuals died along the Oregon Trail alone. If an unexpected blizzard or other severe weather cropped up, the journey could be halted for days on end. Those aleady living in their dugouts or sod-houses could be forced to stay inside for long stretches as well.*

LEFT: *Even less sophisticated than the "soddy" was the dugout, here built by buffalo hunters. Dirt walls are shored up with scrap lumber and buffalo hides cover the plank roof.*
BELOW: *Hunger and disease claimed many young lives; the Andrews family stands at the grave of Willie, aged seven. Ironically, pioneer cemeteries have left patches of prairie undisturbed.*

Around the globe, social and political changes were creating a need and a desire for new, free lands. The Industrial Revolution had led to an improved standard of living in Europe, with a doubling of the population from 1750 to 1850. The resulting shortage of land, coupled with the political turmoil from the failed German democratic revolutions of 1848, had compelled emigrants from scores of German states to the tallgrass prairies of Illinois and Iowa. After the war, many moved farther west into the newly opened western territories, joining newly freed slaves and bankrupt Southern whites. A famine in Scandinavia in the late 1860s was the driving force behind the dividing up and plowing of the prairie lands of Minnesota; the harshness of the northern winters did not deter the hardy Swedes and Norwegians.

The Ukraine and Caucasus, in Southern Russia, sit at the turbulent epicenter of continent-sized weather systems, so their peoples were hardy and flexible, as were the grasses they domesticated for food. Over the centuries, these peoples of the grasslands had developed a hard red winter wheat—Turkey Red. Like other peoples around the world, Mennonites from the Caucasus fleeing religious persecution headed for America, bringing these near-magical seeds to the often harsh climate of Kansas and Nebraska's high plains.

The rest of that country is noticeable primarily for its weather, which is violent and prolonged; its emptiness, which is almost frighteningly total; and its wind, which blows all the time in a way to stifffen your hair and rattle the eyes in your head.

—Wallace Stegner

RIGHT AND FAR RIGHT: *Even during the quiet of a prairie winter, settlers—like their Native American predecessors—worked hard to keep themselves alive. Everything from tinder gathering to quilt making kept them busy every day.*

The moon is the closest of the celestial bodies. But no amount of walking will get you any closer to it. The prairie, in this respect, resembles the moon. The essential feature of the prairie is its horizon, which you can neither walk to nor touch.

—P. Gruchow

Heartache of a Homestead Mother

Julia Louisa Lovejoy, wife of a preacher, followed her husband West in the mid-1850s. While her letters home reflect a time of challenge mixed with hope, the following personal journal entries clearly paint a picture of the heartache endured by many pioneers as they set out for new lands.

Croyden, N.H., Dec. 10, 1854

We are now very busy, making preparations, to go West, in the Spring. We may go to Kansas, if the way opens for us, in the order of Providence. We have "usefulness to our fellow-creatures," in view, before any other object of worldly gain. I am perfectly passive, as it respects "the spot," or state, or Territory where Mr. L. sees fit to pitch his tent, let God direct, and all will be right—I write no more, in this diary, until we reach our place of destination. "Carry us not thence, unless Thy Presence, go with us," is our prayer.

Kansas City, Mo., March 18, 1855

We left Lebanon, N.H., the old paternal home the 6th of March, 1855. O the tears, and heart-agony, as we tore ourselves away from those aged parents, who gave us birth, and those brothers and sisters, so dear to our hearts— we wept until we reached "White River Junction," at Hartford, Vt., where brother Daniel, who accompanied us there, left us and we took the cars. Had a pleasant journey from there to Alton, Ill., in the cars, and thence up the Missouri River, by steam-boat....We landed here at Kansas City Sunday Morning. What a desolate place!

Kansas City, March 28th

Mr. L. left immediately, with Charles Julius, for the Territory, leaving I, and Juliette and Edith, to board at the "American Hotel" in this place, till he could find him a "claim," and erect a cabin on it, for our accommodation. The landlord gives me two dollars per week, for serving, besides boarding me and Edith. Juliette has $1.50 per week, and her board, for waiting on the table. It is very sickly here in this Hotel, and in the Town. Many cases of death. Pneumonia seems to be the prevailing sickness....

April 3rd

All three of us, are sick, and I know we cannot live in this unhealthy atmosphere. Deaths almost, or quite daily, here.... What I can do, I know not, as my children are sick, and I am too unwell to sit up, all the time. No face, I

ever saw before, and if we stay here I fear we shall die. My dear little Edith has been exposed to the measles, and I fear the consequences, as we have not means in our power, to make her comfortable. I must find a private house, if we can, by going about Town, and hire our board, if possible till I can send an express for Mr. L. who is at the Junction of the Big Blue and Kansas Rivers, as he writes me, and he, and his NE Company, have laid out a Town in that spot. They had an excessively hard journey there, and suffered with cold, and snow an occurrence, not common, I am told, in this region. O how my sick lone heart, at this time, sighs for a home, where our children may be comfortable again. What can I do, with but little money, and every thing here so expensive? The price for miserable board here, is $1.00, and $1.50 per day! This is wrong, money is so scarce. I have never seen so much suffering in so short a time, as since I have been here. O how many have left for the Territory who will there find a grave!

April 25th

I left the Hotel, and went to a Mr. West, to board, and whilst I was there, it was announced that the "Financier," a boat, was to sail up the Kansas River to Fort Riley and I immediately engaged passage, and went on board, with my family Juliette being sick, and Edith evidently "coming down" with measles. I wanted if possible to escape from that place of sickness, and death, for I feared that every one of us would die, if we remained there, and our graves be dug by stranger's hand.... If the boat does not start again, for some time, as she has now struck on a sandbar, four miles only from the place, "(K.City)" from whence she started, some way will be provided for us. We are now stopping with a half-breed Indian woman, French Catholic, whose husband lives near the spot, where the boat grounded. Juliette is better, tho' very feeble. Edith is very sick with measles, but patient as a lamb. I have nothing to render her comfortable, in her sickness, and neither suitable food, nor other necessaries, for any of us. I have watched E. day and night, and wept, and prayed, by her bedside, the most of the time, until it seems as tho' nature can sustain but little more, and if I fail, before Mr. L. arrives, what will become of my children, in this condition? I have sent an "express," for Mr. L. and hope he is on his way, to find us. I am straining my eyes continually watching for his coming—why does he delay, when my heart is sinking within me, and I have wept, until the fountain of tears, is nearly exhausted. Must our graves be dug here, and we have no

Christian burial? I cannot rehearse, what I have passed thro, of late, nor need I, for it is written on my heart, in characters, never to be effaced, till I die.

April 28

I can stop here no longer: My little Angel—Edith groans terribly at night, she is in such pain, in her head, and as there is but one room, in the log cabin, where we are, this woman took her bed, and dragged it out on to the porch, to sleep, for "she said she would not sleep in the house, where the child groaned so." I have hired this man for $30 to carry us to the Big Blue, if we do not meet Mr. Lovejoy, on the way.... Edith was evidently failing, and O could I but reach Lawrence, that if she died I might not bury her on the road, or leave here body amongst the Indians.... The next morning, we were on our way at an early hour hoping to reach Lawrence, some time before night, and looking every hour, to meet Mr. L. on the road. I feared Edith had the seal of death, upon her brow. She opened wide, her full blue eye, and looking me full in the face, said she, "Mother, you are good." These were her last words: her voice trembled some, but O so patient—About four o'clock in the p.m. we came in sight of Lawrence, and saw a man approaching us on foot—we held our breath, lest we might be deceived! Lo! 'tis he! We simultaneously uttered a cry, and the next moment, we were sobbing in each other's arms. Mr. L. had arrived in L. an hour previously, and by some means learned that we were near, and run to meet us! O what had we both been thro' since we parted, and there was our dying, idolized child! My God! Why dost Thou suffer this to come upon us!... She does not recognize him—She'll die! This awful truth is forced upon me, and can we survive the awful stroke? She is borne in her father's arms, from the wagon, to the cabin of a kind-hearted Christian family, by the name of Savage, from Hartford, Vt., who have just arrived here. The next day, about two o'clock in the p.m. her spirit went to God—Can I proceed with my mournful story? The next day, May the 5th, we buried her dear little body, at Lawrence, with many tears. This is our first great sorrow, and the billows have quite gone over our soul. I am now about 6 months advanced in pregnancy and why I live, is more than I can tell.

May, the 6th

We tore ourselves from the grave of our loved-one, and sowing our tears along the road, went on our way toward "Big Blue." The third day we reached there, and went into a log cabin, to live with no floor, nor window, and tears were my meat and drink, day and night, until it seemed sometimes as tho' reason, could not retain her throne, unless my sorrows assuaged. No friend that seemed to understand, my sorrow. No acquaintances here, but my family—All is one vast expanse of nature, and tho' the Country is surpassingly beautiful, it is as lonely to me, as tho' I was shut up in a tomb, my heart is so sad, sad—I am glad, I'm born to die.

Manhattan, Oct. 13th

The 17th of Sept. at four o'clock in the p.m. after a lingering and well-nigh death-like sickness, it was announced that "a son was born." A beautiful boy, he truly is, and I have given up to God, to be a "Herald of the Cross," and I feel as tho' the Lord would accept him, and spare his life. My prayer is, that he may be a Samuel, from his birth. "Lord, he is Thine, for time, and for Eternity." I feel the loss of Edith, more and more, O God, let me see my child, in heaven! I thought, and so did my attendants, that I might die in my late sickness, but God, for some purpose hath spared me: may it be to train my little Irving (now four weeks old) for the skies, Lord impart grace.

May 5th, 1856

Great bend of the Blue, in a little cabin, hastily thrown together—this is now our home. We have occupied a "balloon house," so called ready-made, brought on the ill-fated Steamer Hartford, that was burnt to the water's edge, on her downward trip, from Manhattan, to Lawrence. In this house, last Winter, our family, came near freezing, the cold, was so intense. I wrapped my babe in blankets, and my furs, to keep him from perishing, near the stove. Mr. L's station, the first year, was "Fort Riley Mission," and in the fall, was sent to Lawrence station, consequently, we were alone in the winter, and suffered incredibly. O, how I sighed for a comfortable home, in NE again. Mr. L. took him a "claim" adjoining Manhattan, and to prevent its being jumped we have moved on to it, and Mr. L. has been sent by the Lawrence people, to the East, to solicit funds, to build a Church in Lawrence. I am very lonely, in this distant land, and he, so far away, while the political elements, are all in commotion, and war is being threatened. One year ago yesterday, I saw the cold earth, heaped upon the coffin, that contained my darling Edith, and O, what a day, was the anniversary of that heart-rending scene! How my poor lacerated heart, bleeding in every pore, looks to Heaven, that its wounds, may be, (if not healed) made endurable, by the grace of God, bestowed. What a year has been the past! O my weeping days, and nights!... Juliette, was married by her father, the 9th of March, to Dr. L. Whitehorn of Hudson, Michigan. It was a sore trial, to me, to have her marry so young, but I pray the Lord, to bless their union, and bring them, both safe to heaven, at last.

RIGHT: *There are well-documented stories of pioneers going mad from the sound of the winter wind blowing, uninterrupted across the wide prairie, through the cracks of their sodhouses. Women were particularly susceptible to these fits of insanity, as their childcare duties often trapped them inside the house for long periods of time.*

It was late afternoon. A small caravan was pushing its way through the tall grass. The track that it left behind was like the wake of a boat—except that instead of widening out astern it closed in again.

"Tish-ah!" said the grass…"Tish-ah, tish-ah!"…Never had it said anything else—never would it say anything else. It bent resiliently under the trampling feet; it did not break, but it complained aloud every time—for nothing like this had ever happened to it before…."Tish-ah, tish-ah!" it cried, and rose up in surprise to look at this rough, hard thing that had crushed it to the ground too rudely, and then moved on.

—Ole Rolvaag

By the 1870s, hide hunters had virtually eradicated the bison, so the corn and wheat we know today were able to send down their domesticated roots into the black soil that had nurtured the wild prairie grasses for so many thousands of years. The domesticated grasses thrived in the upturned prairie loam: unheard-of yields became commonplace.

But while an overarching view of this time implies progress, individual stories by the thousands were not so happy. A great many of these pioneer homesteaders had been shopkeepers, craftsmen, soldiers, industrial workers, even slaves, before trying their hands at scratching a living directly from their own plots of land. They knew little about farming. Until the crops came up—if they came up—the menfolk often would forage for game away from their homesteads for weeks at a time, leaving their wives and children to fend for themselves. In the vast, treeless stretches of the sea of grass, the wind would howl almost constantly, rains and snows could seem unending, and neighbors were miles away. Their own sanity had to be tightly grasped by those pioneer women who had left far behind a somewhat predictable social order and often a sense of physical security.

Friendship

Out on the prairie, with miles between sodhouses and makeshift towns, neighbors were more than friendly acquaintances. They were lifelines, called on to help in all sorts of situations, from field hand to grave digger, mail carrier to house builder. S.N. Hoisington's mother was often called on to act as a doctor, despite the woman's lack of any kind of formal training. But it was for her companionship, not her healing ways, that a sick woman turned to her in the summer of 1873:

In the summer of 1872 and 73 the gray wolves and coyotes were very numerous. It was not safe to go out across the prairies without a weapon of some kind. My mother was a nurse and doctor combined. In early girlhood she used to help her brother mix his medicines and after she came to Kansas people came for miles for her to doctor their families. She was the only doctor except Dr. Gregg, a pioneer doctor for King City, Kansas.

A man by the name of Johnson had filed on a claim just west of us, and had built a sod house with a shingle roof, wide boards for door frames, and window frames and door made out of flooring lumber. He and his wife had lived there two years, when he went to Salina to secure work. He was gone for two or three months, and wrote home once or twice, but his wife grew very homesick for her folks in the east, and would come over to our house to visit mother. Mother tried to cheer her up but she continued to worry until she got bed fast with the fever. As she grew worse all the time, my mother sent a man on a pony to find her husband, but he failed to locate him. At night she was frightened because the wolves would scratch on the door, on the sod and on the windows,

so my mother and I started to sit up nights with her. I would bring my revolver and ammunition and axe, and some good sized clubs. In the day time my sister would care for her while mother and I went home to rest.

The odor from the sick woman seemed to attract the wolves, and they grew bolder and bolder. I would step out fire off the revolver, and they would settle back for a while, when they would start a new attack. They would stand up on the window sill and look in. I shot one through the window and I found him lying dead in the morning. Finally the woman died and mother laid her out. Father took some wide boards that we had in our loft and made a coffin for her. Mother made a pillow and trimmed it with black cloth, and we also painted the coffin black. After that the wolves were more determined than ever to get in. One got his head in between the door casing and as he was trying to wiggle through, mother struck him in the head with an axe and killed him. I shot one coming through the window. After that they quieted down for about half an hour when they came back again. I stepped out and fired at two of them but I only wounded one. Their howling was awful. We fought these wolves five nights in succession, during which time we killed and wounded four gray wolves and two coyotes.

Old Barney Richards finally found Mr. Johnson, but when he arrived home and found his wife dead and his house badly torn down by wolves he fainted way. He was very grateful to my mother and me for all we had done for his wife and thanked us over and over again. He made me a present of a 15 shot Winchester rifle, improved model. After the funeral, however, he sold out and moved away.

OPPOSITE: *A whitetail doe stands ready to flee if threatened.* **THIS PAGE, CLOCKWISE FROM TOP LEFT:** *Highly adaptable, the great horned owl (Bubo virginianus) is a native of the Americas; the prairie is a feasting ground for the common nighthawk (Chordeiles minor), which feeds off insects on the wing; slender and bright green, the rough green snake (Opheodrys aestivus) prefers the prairie-forest transition areas; wild turkeys (Meleagris gallopavo) were popular game birds for both settlers and Native Americans.*

A Homesteader's Diet

A day filled with hard work should begin and end with a good, hearty meal—and it did, so far as the homesteader could manage. Reality came in the form of crops sacrificed to bad weather, grasshoppers, or fires, provisions running out, and game that was few and far between.

The following accounts are from a few hardy, hungry, and creative foodsmiths:

H.G. Lyons, settler 1856

In the spring of '56 I filed on the claim that is still my home. A shanty 8 x 12, built of dry stone walls, 6 1/2 feet high with slab floor and shake roof's oon followed. This furnished shelter for three of us, my brother, a Mr. Chas Allen—a Massachusetts Yankee—and myself. Things were so unsettled that summer that but little improvement was made. However, we found enough to do to make a living. When fall came and our beloved friends of Missouri shut off our supplies we had only a little corn meal and part of the milk of a young cow to go on.

As it happened, a man named Reese had broken a piece of bottom some two miles from us and planted it to pumpkins, then left. As they were going to waste we helped ourselves. Then for three weeks we lived on mush; about four parts pumpkin and one part corn meal, with a little milk to make it relish. It was all right, for it was the best we could do, but that in no sense compensated for the wear and tear of my stomach, which for years refused to have anything to do with pumpkin pie.

George Flanders, 1857

Father had rented the King Smith farm adjoining the Howard farm on the east, and we raised a pretty good crop and after the corn became suitable for roasting ears—I was detailed as commissary of subsistence for the family—my duties consisted in procuring the materials for the meals for the family—the meals were very much alike in those days—we had no flour or meal or meats except chickens and they were scarce—boiled corn for breakfast, dinner, and supper—when the corn became too hard to boil a grater was made of a sheet of tin bent half-oval and fastened to a narrow board, holes were punched in the tin by a nail and the grater was ready for business, and then all our bread stuff was grated and made into a mush and corn bread, a very agreeable change of diet. This program was carried out three times each day until the corn became too hard to grate—then I shelled it, dried it in the oven and ground it in the coffee mill for each meal—late in the fall times became better politically and financially and I was relieved of my duties of commissary.

Anna Ward, 1860s

Mother Morgan was an honest to goodness Yankee from near Boston, and she baked Boston brown bread and baked beans every Saturday and they were our main dish for Sunday. The hard brown bread crust was used to make coffee; other coffee substitutes were chicory, parched barley, or rye. Our first coffee was the green unroasted coffee and had to be browned in the oven which was a real task to get just brown enough and not burn it. We had no coffee mill so had to pound coffee, spices, etc. in our mortar with a pestle— a tiresome task.

Louisa Prentiss Simpson, 1855

We had that first winter no such thing as eggs. I don't believe there were a dozen hens in the town. No milk. I do not remember seeing a cow. We made our corn meal bread with water, soda and cream-a-tartar, salt and shortening, and ate it with gravy as we had no butter. We had plenty of beans that we boiled, made soup, and baked. We almost lived on beans as that first year we had no potatoes. Our coffee was what they called chicory, made by drying and roasting that vegetable, browning it and grinding it in our grinder.

Susanna Weymouth, 1855

The winter was an extremely cold one, and although I had plenty of fire-wood, and kept the stove red-hot much of the time, I could not prevent the water from freezing in the water bucket, so that we had to break the ice whenever we drank. The bread, being frozen, was generally cut with a hatchet, and thawed out in the oven. I remember that one time John Richie went to Missouri and brought home some apples and potatoes. We had no cellar and placed the bags under the bed, and they froze solid, and remained in that condition as long as they lasted. If a frozen potato is dropped into boiling water and kept boiling until done, the freezing does not appear to injure it. The frozen apples could not be treated in this way, but were thawed out and eaten raw.

> *O…the prairie…its vastness, dreariness, loneliness, is apalling…like the sea on a very smooth day, without beginning or end.*
>
> —Anonymous Englishwoman in Manitoba

Those who found promise in a particular part of Kansas' tallgrass prairie found out all too soon why these Flint Hills were so aptly named. The soil was so full of rocky flint that most of it was virtually impervious to the plow. And although the soil was as rich as in other parts of the prairie, it was much shallower. Huge deposits of limestone lay concealed only inches beneath the surface, acting as a natural rainfall drainage purifier for the frequent rains that blessed the Flint Hills and allowed the grass to grow so tall. But for farmers the limestone was fatal, because plowing open this shallow layer of soil led to nutrient loss and erosion from wind and water. Crops might come up for the first few years, but the land was quickly played out. The Flint Hills of Kansas were covered with broken shards of flint from the retreat of the glaciers thousands of years earlier. The plows could not even begin to be effective.

While small farms hung on and frequently prospered by planting crops in rows throughout most of the former tallgrass prairie from Indiana to Iowa and Minnesota to Missouri, most of the small farmsteads in the Flint Hills were abandoned within a few generations. But the untamed grasslands here were to give a different value to the people of the grass—the production of beef.

ABOVE: *While families on some claims succeeded and stayed to work their land for generations, those toiling in rocky soils found it difficult, if not impossible, to eke out a living.*

LEFT: *When children were not needed to help with the crops, they attended sodhouse schools like this one. While the schoolhouse is relatively large and features corner supports and glass windows, it is made from the same sod bricks used to construct homes.*

RIGHT AND FAR RIGHT: *After just one hundred fifty years on the prairies, American settlers had forever changed the landscape, leaving unplowed only the land that was too rocky for farming. Less than five percent of the original tallgrass prairie remains undisturbed, making it the most endangered ecosystem in North America.*

CHAPTER FOUR

open skies
and cattle drives

Their numbers are few, but the rangeland they manage is vast. By properly caring for one of the largest solar collectors on the planet, they direct the conversion of a huge amount of solar energy into edible energy—protein—for humankind. They are modern-day ranchers.

The best cattle ranchers in the Flint Hills of Kansas and the Osage Hills of Oklahoma regard their ownership of the prairie as a sacred trust—a stewardship of the grasses and the soil that sustains the productivity of the grasses. They avoid using fertilizers, pesticides, or herbicides on prairie land, so to survive economically they must maintain the ecosystem's natural balance in the same way it developed for thousands of years before the introduction of cattle. Their experience over a century and a half is being continuously refined through rigorous scientific analysis by academic experts in range management and biology.

LEFT: *New grasses surround rocky outcroppings at the Konza Prairie Research Natural Area outside Manhattan, Kansas. The prairie survives here only because the soil is too rocky for the plow.*
ABOVE: *A cowboy holds his lasso at the ready as he waits for a signal from his fellow cowpuncher, just visible on the horizon.*

The Dying Cowboy

Oh bury me not on the lone prairie,
Where the wild coyote howls over me,
In a narrow grave, just six by three;
Oh bury me not on the lone prairie.

It matters not, I've oft been told,
Where the body lies if the heart is cold.
Yet grant, oh grant, this wish to me
Oh, bury me not on the lone prairie.

I've always wished to be laid when I died,
In the little churchyard on the green hillside,
By my father's grave there let mine be,
And bury me not on the lone prairie.

Let my death-slumbers be where my mother's prayer
And my sister's tears will mingle there;
Where my friends can come and weep o'er me;
Oh, bury me not on the lone prairie.

'Oh, bury me not,' and his voice failed there,
But they took no heed of his dying prayer.
In a narrow little grave just six by three
They laid him away on the lone prairie.

RIGHT: *Two unidentified cowboys pose for a studio portrait. Because cowhands worked in small groups on ranches far from towns and because of the dangers they faced together on the trail, they often became close friends.*

What is becoming apparent to most range managers is that the seasonal panoply of growth, protein spiking, and decline of the grass is directly related to the historical migratory and forage patterns of the vast herds of bison throughout the prairies.

But as much as their formal understanding of the dynamics of tallgrass prairie soil and grasses has grown, the way in which ranchers "grow" their "crop" has remained a constant: they receive a shipment of cattle and put the animals out into the amazingly nutritious grass; they protect the cattle while they graze; then the ranchers "sweep the pastures" to gather the cattle for shipment to market. In short, modern ranchers mimic with cattle the arrival and departure of the great bison herds. Accomplishing these complex and difficult tasks requires a unique resource, indeed, the very stuff of legend: the cowboy.

From the nineteenth-century dime novel to the silver screens of Hollywood, the American cowboy is perhaps the world's most acknowledged symbol of independence and resourcefulness, the lone rider who answers only to his own code of justice. But this image is faithful to only a few attributes of these remarkable horsemen and horsewomen. The complete picture is much more interesting than the fiction. In actuality, this supposedly quintessential American loner is descended from the traditions of New Spain, and must perform on a daily basis not primarily as an individual but rather as an integral member of a well-choreographed team.

In the course of conquering the Aztec Empire for Spain, Fernando Cortes had in 1519 brought the horse to North America for the first time since its prehistoric ancestor had become extinct—either through climate change or hunting pressure from Paleo-Indians.

LEFT: *Modern-day cowboys herd cattle across the Little Missouri River at Logging Camp Ranch in Amidon, North Dakota. The ranch is made up of both private and public grazing lands.*

By the seventeenth century, New Spain stretched from South America into land that is today California, Arizona, New Mexico, and Texas. Much of these lands were divided into vast ranches, one of whose main functions was the raising of beef cattle. And this was handled by the *vaqueros*.

These rough-and-ready horsemen had to be able to drive the cattle in a herd or venture off to find a single stray head. They had to keep track of this precious commodity from calving to slaughter, helping their *patron* maximize each steer's weight gain. They had to protect the cattle from the hostile environment, unfriendly Indians, and rustlers on the open range.

So, it was in New Spain over the 1700s and early 1800s that the equipment, protective clothing, and downright elegance of style that later came to characterize our familiar cowboy of the American West was invented by these vaqueros, as were the now-familiar tactics of roping and branding individual cows and of moving herds across the landscape.

A Cowboy's Gear

The single most important piece of gear for the drover (a.k.a. cowboy) was not his pistol, it was his saddle. He needed to be certain that it not only connected him to his horse firmly, but also was comfortable for both his mount and himself. Hour upon hour, day after day, of sitting a horse made the comfort and durability of the saddle a must.

The cowboy's hat ranked a close second to his saddle in importance. It had to have a wide brim to protect his face and neck from the sun; the brim could also be pulled down to shield his head from the wind. The fabric needed to be light enough to keep him cool yet dense enough to hold water as he carried it to his cooking pot (hence the term "ten-gallon" hat).

Boots needed to be thick yet flexible—quilting the leather was the answer. The heels were high to help keep feet in the saddle's stirrups, and the boots came halfway up the cowboy's calf to protect him from thorns, brush, and bites from various critters. Spurs were used sparingly so as not to injure the horse, but they were always strapped on the boots for those emergencies when the drover needed that extra "pick-up"—a sudden surge of additional horsepower to avoid a poised rattler or to get out of the way of a stampeding herd of beeves. Leather chaps covered his legs and extended protection up to the waist. Strong leather wrist cuffs and gauntlets protected the forearms and hands, while allowing the drover the ability to handle a thick rope with amazing dexterity.

Sweet Betsy From Pike

Oh, don't you remember sweet Betsy from Pike
Who crossed the big mountains with her lover Ike
With two yoke of oxen, a big yellow dog
And a tall Shanghai rooster and one spotted dog
Singing tooraliooraliooraliay

One evening quite early they camped on the Platte
'Twas near by the road on a green shady flat,
Where Betsy, quite tired, she laid down to repose,
While with wonder Ike gazed on his Pike County rose.
Singing tooraliooraliooraliay

They soon reached the desert, where Betsy gave out,
And down in the sand she lay rolling about,
While Ike, in great tears, he looked on in surprise,
Saying, "Betsy, get up, you'll get sand in your eyes,"
Singing tooraliooraliooraliay

Sweet Betsy got up in a great deal of pain
and declared she'd go back to Pike County again,
Then Ike heaved a sigh and they fondly embraced,
And she traveled along with his arm round her waist.
Singing tooraliooraliooraliay

The Shanghai ran off and the cattle all died.
The last piece of bacon that morning was fried.
Poor Ike got discouraged, and Betsy got mad.
The dog wagged his tail and looked wonderfully sad.
Singing tooraliooraliooraliay

One morning they climbed up a very high hill
And with wonder looked down into old Placerville.
Ike shouted and said, as he cast his eyes down,
"Sweet Betsy, my darling, we've got to Hangtown."
Singing tooraliooraliooraliay

Long Ike and sweet Betsy attended a dance,
Where Ike wore a pair of his Pike County pants.
Sweet Betsy was covered with ribbons and rings.
Quoth Ike, "You're an angel, but where are your wings?"
Singing tooraliooraliooraliay

Long Ike and Sweet Betsy got married, of course,
But Ike, getting jealous, obtained a divorce.
And Betsy, well satisfied, said with a smile,
"There are six good men waiting within half a mile."
Singing tooraliooraliooraliay

These techniques were quickly adapted by those Americans welcomed into Texas in the early 1800s. During this time, much of New Spain rebelled against the Spanish rule and gained independence. Mexico became one of the largest of the former colonies and included in its borders the former territories of New Spain north of the Rio Grande, from Texas west through California. First Texas and then the young United States initiated war with Mexico, and when these had ended in 1848, most of today's Southwestern United States was no longer part of Mexico.

Texan culture, especially, became a unique blend of Mexican and American, but Mexico still did not provide any real market for large numbers of "beeves" on Texas ranches. Fortunately, newer markets were opening to the north. St. Louis and Chicago were now major cities, and the railroad would soon reach from the East Coast all the way to Kansas City.

OPPOSITE: *Indian grass and big bluestem, together with little bluestem and switchgrass, dominate the tallgrass prairie.*

LEFT, TOP: *A group of cowboys bathe the trail dust from their weary bodies. Typically, a drive would last two to three months and cover as many as a thousand miles.*

LEFT, BOTTOM: *Cowboys pose in Denver, Colorado, circa 1900. By this time, cattlemen had learned that a herd could endure cold winters, a discovery that meant cows no longer had to be driven from Texas through the tallgrass, which was rapidly being fenced off and farmed. Ranches sprung up in relatively unpopulated areas like Colorado, Montana, and Wyoming. Note the mixed races in the group—about a quarter of cowboys were African-American and another quarter were Mexican.*

How could people from beautiful enchanting mountains endure life on this flat moor without even a distant hill to look at?… On this great plain it seemed there is nothing to aspire to for long. All poetry and yearning were as though left out of life, or would be smothered if they appeared.

—Iver Bernhard

Perhaps the young, scrawny TexMex cattle ranging one to each hundred acres on the shortgrass of Texas could be driven northward through the tallgrass prairie to reach these markets—and the increasing number of wagon trains moving west on the Oregon, California, and Santa Fe Trails. In the 1840s and '50s, some cattle were driven from Texas to St. Louis, and then shipped by rail to Chicago or even driven to New York City! Some ranchers took their cattle herds as far west as California.

With the approach of the War Between the States, the Border War made Missouri increasingly dangerous for cattlemen. By the outbreak of official hostilities in 1861, most south/north commerce was effectively shut down, including in "Bleeding Kansas," and especially any cattle from Texas, a stalwart of the Confederacy.

But the cessation of hostilities in 1865 meant a ten-fold resumption of the waves of migrants westward—a movement of a tremendous number of people. The Civil War had also greatly sped up the Industrial Revolution in the North, increasing general prosperity and the size of the immigrant population. Small-scale Eastern cattle ranching was rapidly disappearing, and its comparatively mediocre beef had mostly gone to the Union Army for four years, anyway. The resulting demand for good beef now meant a potential ten-fold increase in profits for Texas and Kansas cattlemen who could get their beef to market for sale to cities "Back East."

There had been a wind during the night, and all the loneliness of the world had swept up out of the southwest.

—Wallace Stegner

LEFT: *As spring buds emerge, dry winter grasses that have not yet been burned wave in the chilly wind.*
BELOW: *Women brand cattle, perhaps with an eye for the camera. Every spring and fall, cowhands rounded up the ranch's cattle in order to brand the new calves. Out on the open range, cattle from several different ranches were likely to intermix, necessitating brands for identification purposes.*

Desperately strapped Texas ranchers who had spent years fighting Union soldiers in the east now sent north what little cattle they could round up from their widely dispersed herds. Following trails blazed by Joseph McCoy and Jesse Chisholm, they headed for the proposed railheads that were to connect to St. Louis and Kansas City. 1866 was literally a trailblazing year. It was not a financial success, but the markets took note: the railroads were building and the drovers were learning trail-driving techniques. By 1867 and 1868, the boom was on.

Another major trail north was the Western trail to the mixed grass and shortgrass prairie pasturelands of Western Kansas, Nebraska, Colorado, and Wyoming, where new western boomtowns were springing up. The railroad reached Western Kansas by the late 1860s, so the cattle were destined for the rail towns. The situation was now reversed: at one time, the cattle had arrived because the towns were booming;

now the towns boomed because the cattle were there—and were there in large numbers.

The cowboys—or drovers, as they preferred to be called—were primarily responsible for the health of what was suddenly a very active trade in edible protein. Typically, between one and three thousand head of cattle would be driven in a herd stretching out over two to three miles, for a total journey of 800 to 1,500 miles over a period of two to four months—and overseen by only a dozen or so cowpunchers!

The owner would seldom accompany the herd, so the trail boss, or *caporal*—a term held over from the days of the vacqueros—would post two point drivers at the narrow head of the herd, guiding the half-dozen or so head of cattle that their peers seemed to have chosen to lead them for the entire trail drive. There would be a couple of riders on the flanks of the increasingly wide herd, and the newest cowboys would bring up the "drag" in the rear. The dust alone made that position undesirable, so it usually went to the "greenhorns."

OPPOSITE, TOP:
*Average herds
making their way
to the railtowns of
Kansas numbered
between one and
three thousand
head. Cattle are
said to be able to
smell water from
as far as ten miles
away and could
drink up to thirty
gallons a day.*

OPPOSITE, BOTTOM:
*The chuck wagon
offered cowboys
the few creature
comforts they
received during
the long trail rides.
Despite the tents
pictured here, most
drovers spent their
nights under the
prairie sky. Before
turning in for the
night, the cook
would point the
wagon toward
the North Star,
giving the trail
boss additional
navigational aid
the next morning.*

LEFT: *Autumn grass
grows high at the
Konza Prairie
Natural Resource
Area. Historically,
trees in a tallgrass
prairie grow along
creeks or rivers; fire
keeps the trees few
and far between.*

Home on the Range

Oh, give me a home where the buffalo roam,
Where the deer and the antelope play,
Where seldom is heard a discouraging word,
And the skies are not cloudy all day.

Chorus:
Home, home on the range,
Where the deer and the antelope play,
Where seldom is heard a discouraging word,
And the skies are not cloudy all day.

Oh, give me a land where the bright diamond sand
Flows leisurely down the stream;
Where the graceful white swan goes gliding along
Like a maid in a heavenly dream. Chorus

How often at night, when the heavens are bright
With the light from the glittering stars,
Have I stood there amazed and asked as I gazed
If their glory exceeds that of ours. Chorus

Where the air is so pure, the zephyrs so free,
The breezes so balmy and light,
That I would not exchange my home on the range,
For all of the cities so bright. Chorus

LEFT: *Night falls on the tallgrass prairie, where "big sky" country begins.*
BELOW: *Excitable cattle were especially prone to stampedes at night. Drovers branded the cattle in their care with their own trail brand, as they often herded cattle from more than one owner. Many a drover spent hours in the saddle tracking down a wayward steer or separating cattle from neighboring herds mixed during stampedes.*

OPPOSITE: *Trees are opportunistic, and will take over grasslands if conditions for their growth are right. For this reason, they are called "woody invaders" by grassland scientists.*
LEFT: *Today, cowhands still care for cattle, but their work has been made easier by technology. Although they still spend hours in the saddle, cattle are now transported to market by trucks, so the long trail rides are unnecessary.*

Good drovers actually spent many of their nighttime hours singing to their four-legged charges. The melodic human voices would usually calm a herd that could be stampeded by almost anything from a bolt of lightning to the cracking of a small twig. A stampeding herd was not only very dangerous for the cowpunchers; it could also mean financial loss for the owner. Overnight, the riders would work in five watches of two hours each, so singing would also help keep the cowpunchers awake.

One man would be in charge of the herd of horses: a typical drover would have six to ten horses to use over the course of the drive. Hollywood's emphasis on the cowboy's love of his individual horse was a reflection of a later era, when ranchhands were hired year-round by a specific ranch. At the end of a long trail drive, the horses and wagons would be sold along with the cattle in Abilene or Dodge City. The exhausted drovers would then head east to Kansas City or St. Louis by rail and then

RIGHT: *Cattle graze on rangeland after an ice storm. The cattle originally herded by the Texas cowboys were a hardy breed called Texas longhorns. These cows were descendents of escaped Spanish Criollo cattle, some of which had accidentally mixed with the European breeds raised by Texans at the time. Later, the longhorns were intentionally bred with shorthorns and European breeds to produce a meatier beef.*

south by rail or sternwheeler back home to Texas. While the majority were Caucasian, a significant number of drovers were Hispanic and African-American. The ability to handle your mount and keep your cattle alive and calm were the only qualifications that counted out on the trail.

The chuckwagon was driven by the cook and carried the basic food staples, emergency firewood, water barrels; the few personal possessions of the drovers were carried in their individual bedrolls on the back of their saddles. Since they spent virtually all their waking hours in the saddle, it was their most important possession; saddle sores could be a disabling affliction. To protect from the sagebrush and occasional "timber," chaps for the legs, gauntlets and stiff leather cuffs for the hands and arms, and high-heeled, high-topped, quilted, point-toed boots—all modeled after the Spanish prototypes—were essential. The cowboy's hat was so important—as protection from sun and rain, as a water carrier, as a fire bellows, and as a pillow—that he often spent a couple of months' wages on it. His rifle and pistol were for protection from the occasional renegade Indian band and, more likely, bandits in Missouri and Kansas, especially in the first years after the War.

It so happens that the Chisholm Trail ran just to the west of the Osage Hills of Oklahoma and the Flint Hills of Kansas. The owners and trail bosses who grazed some of these herds briefly in the lush tallgrass began to notice a striking fact: instead of losing weight from the rigors of the trail drive, cattle that traveled through tallgrass prairie actually gained weight. And they did so at an even more remarkable rate if they were put out on that grass in the spring and early summer.

Increased weight meant increased profits. So, over the late 1860s and into the '70s, more and more cattle were driven up first the Shawnee, then the Chisholm, and finally the Western Trail, ending their journey with a few days or even a few weeks in the communal herding areas near the railheads. Railroads had built new spurs to handle the increasing flow to the huge new stockyard facilities springing up in Kansas City, St. Joseph, Omaha, Des Moines, and Chicago. Boom towns sprang up at the railheads to provide permanent chutes for quick loading of the cattle into the rail cars—and various ways for the drovers to spend their just-received pay, from saloons to bathhouses to casinos. In fact, the end-of-trail exuberance and frequent gunplay in Dodge City and Abilene may have been

The Streets of Laredo
or, The Cowboy's Lament

As I walked out on the streets of Laredo,
As I walked out in Laredo one day,
I spied a young cowboy all wrapped in white linen,
All wrapped in white linen as cold as the clay.

"I see by your outfit that you are a cowboy."
These words he did say as I boldly walked by.
"Come sit down beside me and hear my sad story;
I was shot in the breast and I know I must die.

"It was once in the saddle I used to go dashing,
With no one as quick on the trigger as I.
I sat in a card game in back of the barroom,
Got shot in the back, and today I must die.

"Let sixteen gamblers come handle my coffin;
Let sixteen cowboys come sing me a song.
Just take me to Boot Hill and lay the sod o'er me,
For I'm a young cowboy and I know I've done wrong.

"Oh, beat the drum slowly and play the fife lowly,
And play the dead march as you carry my pall.
Put bunches of roses all over my coffin,
Roses to deaden the clods as they fall.

"Go gather around you a crowd of young cowboys
And tell them the story of this, my sad fate.
Tell one and the other before they go further
To stop their wild roving before it's too late.

"Go fetch me a cup, a cup of cold water,
To cool my parched lips," the cowboy then said.
Before I returned, his brave spirit had left him
And gone to its Maker—the cowboy was dead.

We beat the drum slowly and played the fife lowly,
And bitterly wept as we bore him along,
Fore we all loved our comrade, so brave, young, and handsome.
We all loved our comrade although he'd done wrong.

the most dangerous stage of the entire journey for the young cowpokes. Legendary lawmen like Bat Masterson, Wyatt Earp, and Wild Bill Hickok were kept alert by the constant arrivals of large numbers of drovers—most intent on raising Hades after months in the saddle, and perfect marks for gamblers, gunfighters, and "shady ladies."

Hundreds of thousands of head were driven north every year from 1866 to 1885. In 1874 alone, it was estimated that seven and one-half million head were pastured in Kansas, what would soon prove to be an insupportable rate of stocking the land. But the trails from Texas to Kansas were gradually forced westward by increased homesteading from the east, and lured westward by the relentless removal of the Native American tribes from the Great Plains. By the 1890s, railroads also ran from Texas to Kansas, so the cattle could be shipped by rail. The drives were over.

While the cattlemen from Texas, the railroads, and the "commission men" from the stockyards in the big cities were prospering from the East's demand for beef, the small home-steaders whose plows found little arable soil in the Flint Hills tried raising their own small herds of cattle.

Through the years, open herding land across Kansas was gradually fenced in, mostly by the newly invented barbed wire. In the Flint Hills, the bottomland's rich soil was deep, and row crops grew abundantly. But the vast majority of land was the rocky upland, where only cattle grazing was feasible. While a given acre of tallgrass prairie can support many more head than an acre of shortgrass prairie, small acreage still meant a small herd. And if the price went down when your cattle were at their peak weight—as it often did—the small homesteader's choices were to sell at a loss or to keep them on his or her grass. As beef market prices fluctuated on a

Grass is the most widely distributed of all vegetable beings and is at once the type of our life and the emblem of our mortality…the carpet of the infant becomes the blanket of the dead.

—Prairyerth

OPPOSITE: *Bales of hay dot a field along the edge of a Flint Hills access road.*
BELOW: *Cattle in an Oklahoma stockyard await shipment to markets in the East.*

Voices from the Trails

A cowboy's life was both difficult and dangerous, as these colorful reminiscences of life on the trail prove.

Tom Massey

One spring when we were working cattle, we had 3,000 head in one bunch. We got them bedded down but a big cloud was coming up so none of the fifteen men with the herd turned in for any sleep. The cattle were restless and with the first hard clap of thunder they were off. They ran all night and until nearly dark the next day. We boys rode with them through the dark and rain. We could see the lightning on their horns and on the tips of our horses' ears. We tried every way to get them milling, fired our six-shooter in front of them and beat them with our slickers. When they did begin to mill, the ones in the center were crushed to death.

H.P. Cook

The last trip I made "Up the Trail" was in 1874. They were John Chisum's cattle, and were rounded up in Denton and Tarrant counties. It was a big herd, too, at least 3,000. Some said it was 6,000 head, but I don't see how that many could be handled on a drive, unless it was made in two herds. We crossed Red River at Doan's Crossing and took up the Chisolm Trail. I have heard people say over three million head crossed at Doans in one year, but you know, that's a lot of cattle.

We handled the Indians about as usual, paying them a little toll now and then to keep them satisfied. But we had a new experience when we got to the Kansas state line. We ran into a bunch of settlers. The cowboys always called them "nesters." Now, they didn't like for these trail herds to cross their lands at all, and there they were gathered in groups, armed with shotguns and clubs, to force us to narrow the trail down as much as possible and keep the cattle moving. They were afraid they would lose some of their grass. You know, later on the Kansas Legislature passed a law to keep cattle from south of a certain line from being driven at all into their state. They claimed it was to prevent the spread of the so-called "Texas Fever." It was in June of that year that they almost came to war with the cattlemen coming up the trail. There might have been a war, too, but word came through from Washington, granting the Texas cattlemen the right to drive their cattle through the Indian Territory, and to the Kansas market....

Jesse Jolly

We were camped near a stream of water when a loud clap of thunder sent the cattle on a stampede. I mounted my horse to keep them from running off of a bluff into the creek, and my horse turned a complete somersault down into the water, throwing me against a cottonwood tree. I thought I was on a limb up in the tree, when a flash of lightning showed me that I was on the ground with my feet locked around the tree trunk. I kept my seat until the cattle had gone on past me. There were about twelve of us with the outfit and they really did rawhide me about being on the ground and thinking I was safe up in the tree.

grand scale, small ranchers often were forced to keep their cattle grazing year-round. Overgrazed, the grasses' belowground growth tips became damaged. The grass soon lost its seemingly magical ability to rejuvenate.

The rest of the vast, deep-soiled reaches of tallgrass prairie—from Texas to the prairie provinces of Canada—had been plowed under for row-crop agriculture. The bison had been slaughtered for their hides or for meaningless sport. Only in the Flint Hills and Osage Hills did ranching remain dominant. But it would take decades of trial and error by cattlemen and exhaustive scrutiny by scientists to determine that the key is not to concentrate on raising cattle but rather on raising grass. The health of the dominant four species of warm-weather grasses is determined by the intricate symbiosis among grazers, grasses, soils, insects, other wildlife, and even below-ground fungi: in short, the natural balance of the entire tallgrass prairie biome.

It is said that the best way to evaluate the health of the prairie is neither from a motorized vehicle nor an airplane. It is not even on foot. The height and point-of-view of a rider on horseback is ideal. So even as the huge trail drives gradually faded into history, the cowboys remained a

crucial component of the cattle business. Many became more or less permanently employed by one or several ranches. Their experience on the Great Plains helped their employers to develop their understanding of the seasonal cycles of the grasses, water, fire, and grazing—all the elements that keep the prairie in balance. As the smaller landholders in the Flint Hills gradually gave up fighting the markets and sold out to the larger outfits, land consolidation allowed for large enough herds of cattle to allow continuous monitoring of the vitality of the grasses over long periods of time. Dominant theories of range management became lore.

In the last third of the twentieth century, biologists, botanists, and range management experts have begun to understand the correlation between what the Native Americans had observed with the bison and what the cowboys of the remaining tallgrass prairie were prescribing for the health of their animals. The main requirement is still simply listening to the prairie.

OPPOSITE: *Texas longhorns are herded onto a railcar in Abilene, Kansas, which boomed as a "cow town."*
ABOVE: *Ranchland is visited by the two things that keep a tallgrass prairie healthy and vibrant: grazers and fire.*

grasslands for a global community

Some of the most comprehensive studies of grasslands occurring anywhere on the planet are being conducted at the Konza Prairie Research Natural Area in Manhattan, Kansas. Located in the northern reaches of the Flint Hills, Konza Prairie is owned by the noted environmental organization The Nature Conservancy, and is administered by the Division of Biology of Kansas State University. Grassland scientists and researchers from around the world are coming to Konza to "listen to the prairie" and to learn from and collaborate with Konza's internationally recognized experts in prairie ecosystems and management. Just a few miles down the road, University of Kansas is using global imaging from satellites orbiting miles above the Earth to monitor ecosystem-wide changes in grassland biomes as diverse as the tallgrass prairie of the Flint Hills and the steppes of Mongolia.

One of the first research sites funded through the National Science Foundation's Long-Term Ecological Research program, Konza Prairie is 8,600 acres, divided into scores of discrete research grass plots. One plot may be burned annually, the next biannually, another every five years, and yet another every twenty. One large study site may be burned annually but grazed for three months out of the year by cattle, its neighbor burned annually and grazed year-round by bison. In some cases, it has taken decades for conclusive evidence to be collected about differing management practices. After all, it took the tallgrass prairie ten thousand years to lay down its amazingly fertile soil.

LEFT: *Only proper stewardship and a commitment to learning more about the functioning of a healthy grassland can save the remaining tallgrass prairies.*

There is a look about men who come from sojourning in that country, as if the sheer nakedness of the land had somehow driven the soul back upon its elemental impulses.

—Mary Auston

Botanists observe the effects of varying these fire and grazing patterns on the grasses. Agronomists quantify the amount of carbon that both native tallgrasses and human-engineered row crops pull out of the atmosphere and deposit into the soil. Hydrologists study the impact of cattle and bison hooves on stream banks; entomologists record the occurrence of new species of insects—the tallgrass is home to scores of different types of grasshoppers alone! Ornithologists ponder the declining populations of ground-nesting birds in open prairie.

In one area covering several acres are large translucent metal and plastic structures that are used to manipulate the timing and amount of rain that falls onto the grasses below. Potential global climate change could alter the rainfall on the prairie; this experiment may yield information

LEFT: *The coyote, also known as the prairie wolf, is just one of the prairie's wild denizens. A night hunter, the coyote preys mainly on rodents and hares, but will also eat carrion as well as a wide range of animal and vegetable matter.*

about the possible effects of such climate changes. Nearby, graduate students slip long, flexible fiberoptic lines several meters into the ground, down a clear plastic tube. At the far end of the line is a tiny camera lens, at the other a video recorder.

The lens is pulled up a pre-set diagonal course, stopping at regular intervals every few inches, the exact depths dutifully logged. Resulting videotape is compared at each stop to that exact same spot each previous month. What emerges over a period of years is a comprehensive view of a world that does nothing less than support our lives on this planet. The all-important growth buds and incredibly intricate root systems of the dominant native grasses and their less dominant cousins, scores of species of wildflowers—known to scientists as forbs—are examined in relation to the simultaneous data on climatic fluctuations, grazing patterns, and fire events gleaned from those controlled plots. Revealed are the intricate activities of nematodes—billions of tiny worms, some of which, together with a seemingly infinite number of microscopic mycorrhizal fungi, allow plant roots to draw sustenance from the soil and pass valuable fertilizing minerals back again.

The results of these and other investigations are the scientific basis for specific proposals to scientists, ranchers, and conservationists, all of whom are working toward the goal of understanding and conserving North America's tallgrass prairie. These scientific observations can also provide valuable comparisons for farmers, for whom soil conservation is increasingly crucial—after all, many of their crops are domesticated

OPPOSITE, TOP:
*Property that was
formerly the Z-Bar
Ranch is now part
of the Tallgrass
Prairie National
Preserve, a joint
project by the
National Park Trust
and the National
Park Service. The
historic limestone
barn was built in
1911.*
OPPOSITE, BOTTOM:
*The nineteenth-
century limestone
house, with the
barn formerly part
of the Z-Bar Ranch,
now houses a
visitors' center
and bookstore.*
LEFT: *The Lower
Fox Creek school, a
nineteenth-century
one-room school-
house, also sits on
the grounds of the
Tallgrass Prairie
National Preserve.*

Nature abhors an elevation as much as it abhors a vacuum; a hill is no sooner elevated than the forces of erosion begin tearing it down. These prairies are quiescent, close to static; looked at for any length of time, they begin to impose their awful perfection on the observer's mind. Eternity is a peneplain.

—Wallace Stegner

grasses, their soil created by the prairie grasses over thousands of years. Repeated plowing and use of pesticides and herbicides on former prairie lands for the purpose of growing row crops may be depleting the mineral content of the soil, exacerbating wind and water erosion and resulting in polluted streams and rivers. Understanding how a healthy prairie functions at the microbial level may be invaluable in guiding sustainable agricultural practices in the future.

The human population of the planet continues to grow. Governments are under pressure to convert their remaining grasslands to row crop agriculture and to increase their grazing herds to provide more protein in their peoples' diets. Should China increase its yak herds on the Mongolian steppes? Should Kenya open vast reaches of the Serengeti for small-plot row crop farming?

By observing and creating their own experiments on the soil and grasses that have been spared both the plow and overgrazing, scientists from around the world can adapt the Konza techniques to help the endangered steppes of the Ukraine, Mongolia, and Siberia, the pampas of Argentina, the lowland grasslands of Australia, and the vast African veldt. Using the Flint Hills of Kansas as a laboratory, they are joining their North American colleagues in developing informed positions on such issues as plant biodiversity and invasions by non-native species.

But how should a healthy prairie be defined? What point in the long history of the tallgrass should we be trying to replicate? Should a healthy prairie be considered in the framework of post-European settlement? Or should it be defined according to its pre-Columbian nature? Perhaps post-glacial is better? Is it feasible, or even biologically intelligent, in today's largely post-prairie farm- and rangelands to attempt to tear down fences throughout huge tracts of the Midwest and West and reintroduce vast migratory herds of bison and swathes of native grasses to replace cattle and much of the wheat and corn belts?

RIGHT: *Today, fires like this one at the Konza Prairie Research Natural Area at Kansas State University are carefully prescribed and managed.*

OPPOSITE, TOP: *A Konza Prairie crew rides a new high-powered water-pumping truck during the spring burn season.*

OPPOSITE, BOTTOM: *This worker lights a backfire using a drip torch. Note the chert (a fine-grained quartz), typical of the Flint Hills region, exposed by the fire.*

Many Konza scientists have concluded that prairie biomes are best characterized by maximum coverage by a few dominant species of grasses, with fewer forbs and minimal woody species. Early European settler accounts sometimes describe grasses waving as high as a horse's withers, while others talk of a monotonous low expanse. Nature's and Native Americans' uncontrolled burns on the prairie were the determining factor in what was actually a patchwork of grasses at varying heights, depending on how recently they had burned. Now, so many trees grow at the edge of the remaining tallgrass that regular burns are essential—without it, woody invaders would encroach rapidly, guaranteeing the disappearance of our glorious grasslands within a generation. Scientists estimate that a significant tract of good soil, even if properly re-seeded and religiously tended, would require at least several hundred years before it would once again become a fully functioning prairie with its complete array of organisms and processes. So to let it be overrun is a virtual writ of extinction.

It is our responsibility to act as stewards of what remains of the open grasslands and to protect the precious soils it has created everywhere in the world. We must finally come to understand that every major ecosystem in the world has tremendous economic, political, and social value to humankind. If we could come to recognize the importance of natural capital, we might be able to quantify such a global measurement of ecosystem services—nothing less than the air we breathe, the food we eat, and yes, the peace we feel in its glorious presence.

Nonfiction

Andrist, Ralph K. *The Long Death: The Last Days of the Plains Indians.* University of Oklahoma Press, 2001.

Bailey, Garrick A. *The Osage and the Invisible World: From the Works of Francis La Flesche.* University of Oklahoma Press, 1999.

Callahan, Alice Anne. *The Osage Ceremonial Dance I'n-Lon-Schka.* University of Oklahoma Press, 1993.

Chapman, Kim Alan, Adelheide Fischer, and Mary Kinsella Ziegenhagen. *Valley of Grass: Tall Grass Prairie and Parkland of the Red River Valley.* North Star Press, 1999.

Heat-Moon, William Least. *PrairyErth: A Deep Map.* Houghton Mifflin Company, 1991.

Hoy, Jim. *Cowboys and Kansas: Stories from the Tallgrass Prairie.* University of Oklahoma Press, 1997.

Hubalek, Linda K. *Butter in the Well: A Scandinavian Woman's Tale of Life on the Prairie.* Butterfield Books, 1994.

Jones, Harlo. *O Little Town: Remembering Life in a Prairie Village.* University of Manitoba Press, 1995.

Jones, Stephen R. *The Last Prairie: A Sandhills Journal.* McGraw-Hill, 2000.

Kindscher, Kelly. *Edible Wild Plants of the Prairie: An Ethnobotanical Guide.* University Press of Kansas, 1987.

Kindscher, Kelly. *Medicinal Wild Plants of the Prairie: An Ethnobotanical Guide.* University Press of Kansas, 1992.

Kinsey, Joni Louise. *Plain Pictures: Image of the American Prairie.* Smithsonian Institution Press, 1996.

Kirt, Russel R. *Prairie Plants of the Midwest: Identification and Ecology.* Stipes Publishing Co., 1995.

Ladd, Douglas. *Tallgrass Prairie Wildflowers.* Falcon Publishing Company, 2000.

Manning, Richard. *Grassland: The History, Biology, Politics, and Promise of the American Prairie.* Penguin, reprint edition, 1997.

Muller, Mark. *Prairie in Your Pocket: A Guide to the Plants of the Tallgrass Prairie.* University of Iowa Press, 2000.

Murphy, Timothy. *Set the Ploughshare Deep: A Prairie Memoir.* Ohio University Press, 2000.

Packard, Stephen, the Society for Ecological Restoration Conference, William R. Jordan, and Cornelia F. Mutel. *The Tallgrass Restoration Handbook: For Prairies, Savannas, and Woodlands.* Island Press, 1997.

Reichman, O.J. *Konza Prairie: A Tallgrass Natural History.* University Press of Kansas, 1991.

Samson, Fred B., Fritz L. Knopf, and E. Benjamin Nelson. *Prairie Conservation: Preserving North America's Most Endangered Ecosystem.* Island Press, 1996.

Shirley, Shirley. *Restoring the Tallgrass Prairie: An Illustrated Manual for Iowa and the Upper Midwest.* University of Iowa Press, 1994.

Smith, Annick. *Big Bluestem: Journey into the Tall Grass.* Council Oak Distribution, 1996.

Taylor, Colin F. *Buckskin and Buffalo: The Artistry of the Plains Indians.* Rizzoli, 1998.

Zimmerman, John L. *The Birds of Konza: The Avian Ecology of the Tallgrass Prairie.* University Press of Kansas, 1993.

Fiction

Cather, Willa. *My Antonia.* Houghton Mifflin, reprint edition, 1995.

Cather, Willa. *O, Pioneers!* Houghton Mifflin, reprint edition, 1997.

Rolvaag, Ole Edvart. *Giants in the Earth.* HarperCollins, reprint edition, 1999.

Nonfiction for Children

Holt, Faye Reineberg. *Homemade Fun: Games and Pastimes of the Early Prairies.* Fitzhenry and Whiteside Ltd., 1999.

Hook, Jason. *American Plains Indians.* Osprey Publishing Co., 2000.

Johnson, Rebecca. *A Walk in the Prairie.* Carolrhoda Books, 2000.

Lee, Evelyn. *Bluestem Horizon: A Story of a Tallgrass Prairie.* Soundprints Corp., 1998.

Fiction for Children

Brink, Carol. *Caddie Woodlawn.* Aladdin Paperbacks, reprint edition, 1997.

MacLachlan Patricia. *Sarah, Plain and Tall.* HarperCollins Juvenile Books, 1985.

Turner, Ann. *Dakota Dugout.* Aladdin Paperbacks, 1989.

Wilder, Laura Ingalls. *Little House on the Prairie.* HarperTrophy, first Harper edition, 1973.

Worcester, Donald Emmet. *Cowboy with a Camera: Erwin E. Smith, Cowboy Photographer.* Amon Carter Museum, 1998.

ORGANIZATIONS

Center for Grassland Studies
222 Keim Hall
PO Box 830953
University of Nebraska-Lincoln
Lincoln, NE 68583-0953
402-472-4101
www.grassland.unl.edu

Iowa Prairie Network
1308 160th Avenue
Knoxville, IA 50138

Missouri Prairie Foundation
Box 200
Columbia, MO 65205

The Nature Conservancy
www.tnc.org

Northern Prairie Wildlife Research Center
8711 37th Street Southeast
Jamestown, ND 58401
701-253-5500
www.npwrc.usgs.gov

Sierra Club
85 Second Street, Second Floor
San Francisco, CA 94105-3441
415-977-5500
www.sierraclub.org

Tallgrass Ontario
659 Exeter Road
London, Ontario N5Y 2R7
Canada
www.tallgrassontario.org

VISITING THE PRAIRIE

Following is a selected list of prairie preserves that are open to visitors.

Colorado Tallgrass Prairie Natural Area
Boulder, CO
cnap.state.co.us

Goose Lake Prairie State Natural Area
Park Office
5010 N. Jugtown Road
Morris, IL 60450
815-942-2899

Hole-in-the-Mountain Prairie
Lake Benton, MN
Contact: The Nature Conservancy
1313 5th Street SE
Minneapolis, MN 55414I

Illinois Nature Preserves Commission
(Provides information on prairie preserves
   in Illinois)
6000 North Grand Avenue West
Springfield, IL 62706

Jeffers Petroglyphs Historic Site
27160 Couty Road 2
Comfrey, MN 56019
507-628-5591

Konza Prairie Research Natural Area
Manhattan, KS
913-532-6620
www.tnc.org

Midewin National Tallgrass Prairie
30071 South State Route 53
Wilmington, IL 60481
815-423-6370
www.fs.fed.us/mntp/

Ojibway Prairie Complex
Windsor, Ontario
Canada
www.city.windsor.on.ca./ojibway/complex.htm

Tallgrass Prairie National Preserve
Rt. 1, Box 14
Strong City, KS 66869
316-273-8494
e-mail: *tapr interpetation@nps.gov*

Tallgrass Prairie Preserve
PO Box 458
Pawhuska, OK 74056
918-287-4803
www.tnc.org

©Tom Bean: 3, 9, 10, 20, 30–31, 32, 33, 40–41, 42, 45, 53, 56 top left, 56 bottom left, 56 bottom right, 79, 80–81, 82–83, 94–95, 96, 97 bottom left, 100, 101, 105, 119, 128 bottom, 138–139

©Richard Day/Daybreak Imagery: 18, 34 top left

Dembinsky Photo Associates: ©Skip Moody: 128 center

From the Collection of Gilcrease Museum, Tulsa, OK: 106–107 ("The Stampede" by Frederic Remington)

Kansas State Historical Society: 74, 84 left, 87 top, 90, 99 bottom, 104, 109 top

Library of Congress: 39 right, 63 top left, 64, 68 bottom, 69, 71 right, 72 top, 107 right, 114 top, 114 bottom, 124; ©Edward Curtis: 46 left, 49 right, 62, 63 right

©Minnesota Office of Tourism: 44

National Anthropological Archives, Smithsonian Institute: 68 top

National Archives: 54 bottom, 59 right, 60, 80 bottom, 83 top, 103 right, 113 right

Nebraska State Historical Society, Solomon D. Butcher Collection: 77, 78, 80 top, 83 bottom, 87 bottom, 99 top, 109 bottom, 117 right

©James Nedresky: 1, 2, 6 all, 11, 12–13, 17, 19, 24, 26–27, 28–29, 36 left, 38–39, 46–47, 48–49, 50–51, 52, 54 top, 56 center left, 56–57, 58–59, 61, 70–71, 76, 84–85, 88 left, 88–89, 92–93, 102–103, 108, 112–113, 115, 120, 122, 125, 126–127, 128 left, 129, 132 top, 132 bottom, 132–133, 134, 135, 136, 137 top, 137 bottom, endpapers

North Wind Picture Archives: 43 top, 72 bottom

©Jerry Pavia: 37 left

©Harvey Payne: 14, 21, 35, 36 top right, 37 top right, 97 top left, 97 top right, 97 bottom right, 110–111, 116–117, 128 top right, 130–131

©Larry Schwarm: 25

©Ty Smedes: 16, 34 top right, 36 bottom right, 56 top right

Smithsonian American Art Museum/Art Resource, NY: 43 bottom, 67

©Smithsonian Institution, 2000: 22–23 (Mural by Hugh McKay, McKay/Scheer Studios)

South Dakota Art Museum Collection: 73 ("Homesteader's Wife" by Harvey Dunn)

Western History Collection, University of Oklahoma Library: 63 bottom left, 121, 123

Willard Clay Photography, Inc.: 55, 86; ©Scott R. Avetta: 34 bottom left; ©Joseph Kayne: 37 bottom right; ©Ruth Hoyt: 34 bottom right, 118

DIARY CREDITS

The writers would like to pass on a special thanks to the Kansas State Historical Society's Kansas Museum of History, Topeka, Kansas.

Bingham, Anne E., "Sixteen Years on a Kansas Farm," *Collections of the Kansas State Historical Society,* 1919–1922, vol. 15, pp. 501-523.

Chief Curly Head speech from the Edward Everett Dale Collection, Western History Collections, University of Oklahoma.

Combes, Emily, unpublished letters, 1871, typed copies, History, Rice County, Library and Archives Division, Kansas State Historical Society, Topeka, Kansas.

Flanders, George E., 1857, handwritten, Early Kansas Reminiscences, History, Shawnee County, Old Settlers Association, Library and Archives Division, Kansas State Historical Society, Topeka, Kansas.

Hoisington, Mrs. Hannah C. Miller, "A Thrilling Experience with Wolves," Lilla Day Monroe Collection of Pioneer Stories, Library and Archives Division, Kansas State Historical Society, Topeka, Kansas.

Lovejoy, Julia, Diary, 1828–1864, microfilm, MS 802, Library and Archives Division, Kansas State Historical Society, Topeka, Kansas.

Lyons, Horace G., 1856, typed reminiscence, History, Shawnee County Old Settlers, 1908, Library and Archives Division, Kansas State Historical Society, Topeka, Kansas.

Moore, Ely, Jr., "A Buffalo Hunt with the Miamis in 1854," *Transactions of the Kansas State Historical Society,* 1907–1908, vol. 10, pp. 402–409.

Simpson, Louisa B. (Prentiss), Reminiscence, "Grandmother Letters," Collection Simpson, Library and Archives Division, Kansas State Historical Society, Topeka, Kansas.

Snell, Joseph W., editor, "Roughing It On Her Kansas Claim: The Diary of Abbie Bright," *Kansas Historical Quarterly,* Autumn, 1971 and Winter, 1971.

Ward, Anna Morgan, Reminiscences. Special thanks to the Ward family.

Weymouth, Susannah, Reminiscence of her early life in Topeka, 1855, typed copy, History, Shawnee County Old Settlers Association, Library and Archives Division, Kansas State Historical Society.